What people are saying about
Letting Glow

A thoroughly insightful and engaging read! Phill's relatable authentic self shines through, whilst he makes spirituality and the unfoldment of psychic senses accessible to us all. A wonderful book for anyone embarking on a pathway to spiritual enlightenment through seeking understanding of the spirit dimensions of life.

Claire Broad, Medium, Spiritual Teacher and Author of *What the Dead are Dying to Teach Us* (Watkins) and *Answers from Heaven* (Piatkus)

Letting Glow is a very unique book. Part guide, part soulful journey through grief, an amazing investigation into the spirit world at a comforting level. Highly recommended.

Shannon Sylvia, *Ghost Hunters International* (SyFy Channel), *Paranormal State* (A&E Network), *My Horror Story* (Travel Channel)

Letting Glow

a guide to intuition, spirituality,
and living consciously

Letting Glow

a guide to intuition, spirituality,
and living consciously

Phill Webster

BOOKS

Winchester, UK
Washington, USA

JOHN HUNT PUBLISHING

First published by O-Books, 2023
O-Books is an imprint of John Hunt Publishing Ltd., 3 East St., Alresford,
Hampshire SO24 9EE, UK
office@jhpbooks.com
www.johnhuntpublishing.com
www.o-books.com

For distributor details and how to order please visit the 'Ordering' section on our website.

Text copyright: Phill Webster 2022

ISBN: 978 1 80341 220 7
978 1 80341 221 4 (ebook)
Library of Congress Control Number: 2022934750

A CIP catalogue record for this book is available from the British Library.

Design: Stuart Davies

UK: Printed and bound by CPI Group (UK) Ltd, Croydon, CR0 4YY
Printed in North America by CPI GPS partners

We operate a distinctive and ethical publishing philosophy in
all areas of our business, from our global network of authors to
production and worldwide distribution.

Contents

Dedication

For my mum, Maureen Webster, for everything that you did for me while you were physically here, and everything you continue to do for me in Spirit. In passing over, you transformed us both. Thank you for always being near. My love forever.

Acknowledgements

My love to Laura, my wife to be, for supporting, loving, and believing in me.

Special thanks to Claire Broad, for introducing me to, and teaching me about mediumship.

To Gilly Hall, for my first development circle, and everyone at Barnes Healing Church.

To Sam for always being there, and to Deb & Martin, Kyle Newton, Matt, Mingo, Danny, Ronja, Sanj, Jo, Cosmin, and Paul.

To the team at O-Books, thanks for the encouragement and for taking on a first-time author.

Introduction

January 14th, 2021

The phone was ringing, waking me up. 7.50am. Who could be calling me at that time? It was a bit early for my mum to call. Perhaps she wanted to add more food to the home deliveries that I'd organized, perhaps she just wanted to chat and assumed I would be up. But it wasn't her number that flashed on my phone. This wasn't good.

"Hello?"

Katy. My mum's next-door neighbor. I didn't know her so well.

"Phill, have you spoken with your mum this morning? The carers can't get in."

The carers. Nurses that had been going to my mum's house for a couple of months to make sure she took her meds in the right order. At 76, with a heart condition, high blood pressure, and after a year of isolating at home through 2020 due to the COVID-19 crisis, she'd had a period of becoming confused due to being out of her usual routine. They couldn't get in because they didn't have a key, and they didn't have a key because a couple of weeks earlier, my mum had become spooked, telling me that someone had been knocking on the door late at night. She didn't feel comfortable about the spare key being left in the security box on the doorstep. So I'd suggested that she should take it in if it made her feel safer. I deeply regretted that decision now.

They'd called an ambulance but it was forty minutes away. The Isle of Wight has limited resources. And due to a new Coronavirus variant that had surfaced in the UK through the winter, the island's elderly population were dwindling fast.

I ended the call and immediately dialed my mum's home number. It kept ringing. I called her mobile phone. It continued to ring out.

Laura, my fiancée, was awake beside me and concerned.

"It's different this time," I said to her, sitting on the edge of the bed and continuing to call both phones. What I didn't say was why I knew it was different. I thought about the face I'd seen the night before, the other person with my mum on our video call before I'd gone to bed.

"Are the carers there right now?" I'd asked her, after seeing a man with thinning hair and glasses leaning in over her phone when she'd answered it.

"No," she'd replied, and went on to complain about them as she'd done most nights recently. She had been returning to normal at a fast rate, no more confusion, getting increasingly annoyed at the unwanted company coming to the house three times a day and treating her with what she felt was condescendence.

"Wait a minute, Mum," I'd said. "Sorry to interrupt. But are you telling me that there's absolutely no one with you in the house right now?"

"No," she replied again dismissively. "They were here at dinnertime and being a bloody nuisance."

Why had I so easily dismissed that? I knew what I'd seen. A man. Plain as day. Leaning over her phone and taking up the entire screen just as she had answered the FaceTime call. And then he'd gone, and she'd said no one was there. And I had believed her. No one visited except the carers, for ten minutes at a time and at their allotted schedule, and our phone call had been quite late at night. My logical brain told me that I had made a mistake, that I hadn't seen a man with thinning grey hair, glasses, and a surgical mask pulled beneath his nose. How could I have done if there was no one else there? It hadn't made sense, so my brain simply banished it.

And now she wasn't answering her phones or the door. And she was on the Isle of Wight and I was in London, helpless to do anything.

"I've got to go there," I said to Laura, immediately dressing and grabbing some spare clothes to put in a bag. We didn't have transport to get that far. I owned an electric motorbike but the range would barely get me south of London.

My phone rang again. Katy.

"The fire brigade are here," she said. "They've gotten in and she's laying on the floor, they're trying to resuscitate her."

I hung up and stupidly began calling my mum's phone again. Someone switched it off. A couple of minutes later one of the nurses called. My mum was gone.

Laura let out a wail beside me. I think I probably cried.

Chapter One

Early Signs

When I was a kid, around eight or nine, I was roaming the streets one afternoon with another friend of mine. I remember exactly where we were when I posed a question to him. We were in a narrow alley that connected back gardens in the local neighborhood. I don't remember what we were doing around there. Possibly looking to get into mischief. Maybe scouting for good hide and seek spots.

"Do you ever get this feeling," I'd asked him, and realized I didn't quite know how to articulate what was on my mind. "Like, I am me?" It was the only way I could think of putting it.

"Yeah," he'd answered immediately.

I didn't believe him. I knew I hadn't asked the question properly. But I didn't know how to better explain it. I tried again.

"It's like, I know I'm me, but I'm also like, another me." I still didn't know how to convey what was on my mind.

Again he agreed. He said he knew exactly what I meant. I suspected that he didn't. There wasn't really anything else to say.

I'd grown up an only child. Loved unconditionally by my mum. I mean everyone's got their mother's love if they're lucky enough. But she really, really loved me. She'd been a lonely woman. She'd had the hardest of upbringings. Born on June 27th, 1944, her own mother had passed away from breast cancer when my mum was only eleven. She'd never gotten over it. She still cried about it the last time I saw her. People had taken advantage of her throughout her life. My dad. My stepdad. Other boyfriends. She hadn't had an intimate relationship for the last twenty years of her life. We spoke every day. Even when

4

I lived abroad from my twenties to my forties, we called each other pretty much daily.

When I was a kid she'd encouraged me to explore my imagination. I loved movies. It was the early 80s and *Star Wars*, *Superman* and *E.T.* were all the rage. I wanted to be an actor. A stuntman. Anything exciting and anything involving working in the film industry. I would watch the documentary *The Making of The Empire Strikes Back* repeatedly on VHS. We went on a trip to London when I was six to see *The Sound of Music* with Petula Clark in the West End. I wouldn't leave my seat during the interval in case it started again before I could get back. I instantly had a crush on one of the girl actors in the von Trapp family. I decided right then and there that a life in the arts was for me.

From an early age I'd tapped into something straight off the bat. Life was meant to be fun. Life was supposed to be an adventure. Life was in everything. I'd speak to every tree I passed in the mornings on my walk to school. My dog Lucy would escort me there, following a few paces behind or in front. Then she'd come and pick me up again of her own accord later in the afternoon. A wonderful dog. A crossbreed Boxer/Collie. She was my best friend. My parents would let her out into the garden and she would repeatedly escape, roaming the streets before picking me up from school, and back home for dinner. Despite difficult things going on around me, such as an alcoholic father who would regularly physically assault my mum, I had a very vibrant and innate sense of a purposeful inner world that was just as real as the outer world, and maybe even better. These two worlds would blend seamlessly into one.

Eventually, my mum decided she'd had enough of being a punching bag, and wanted to get away from my dad and somewhere safe. I remember waking one night to her climbing into my bed, and hearing my dad yelling drunkenly from their bedroom that he was going to attack her. I'd never heard him speak like that before. I'd witnessed the violence, but I don't remember it now. Hearing him say those things to her shocked and scared me.

We left Derby when I was eight, the place where I was born, and went to live on the Isle of Wight with an old flame of hers. An older man, who had a teenage son. I tried to roll with the punches, but it was hard. This man was a very different man to my dad. Despite his abuse towards my mother, my biological father had always been kind to me directly. Now, I can't forgive the things he did to her, but when things were good with them, things were *really* good with all of us.

This new man was different. For starters, he seemed to be jealous of my relationship with my mum. In hindsight, I realize that he saw me as a threat. He was in his fifties but already an old man. He was very old-fashioned. He had asthma and claimed he was allergic to dogs, so we'd had to leave Lucy behind. He called me "boy" instead of by my name, he would lock me out of the flat on the weekends despite me finding it very hard to make new friends. All the local kids thought my accent was weird and based on that they decided that they didn't want to know me. For the first time, that inner world I mentioned earlier began to feel less real. The outer experiences were taking over. Living with this strange man who didn't want me there. Trying to make friends with the local kids who didn't want to know me. Starting a new school and having similar problems there. A bully for a stepbrother. At least I had a few toys I could play with and get lost in a fantasy world on my own. But one night I remember playing with a couple of He-Man figures on the floor in the hallway of the small flat we now lived in. My stepdad came out of the living room, and after intimidatingly watching me play for awhile, berated me for talking to myself and playing with "dolls". He really was such a dick.

So naturally, I evolved and adapted to my surroundings.

I changed my accent, so as to be accepted by the local kids.

It worked, although I never felt fully integrated with them. My idiot stepfather insisted that I call him dad, so I did, if only to keep the peace and achieve some sort of acceptance from him. We moved across the road to a new council house being built in the mid-eighties. I had friends, but in my desperate attempts to be accepted, I began playing the fool at school, and soon became relegated to the desk at the front of the class right next to the teacher. I developed a keen interest in the esoteric. Books on ghosts, movies about vampires or anything supernatural, I became obsessed with these things. I found it easier to escape in the pages of a fantastical book or a movie than deal with my life at the time. My teachers noticed this and pointed out how such interests would never serve my future. And of course, my stepdad insisted I was a loser. Why wasn't I interested in joining the army like my stepbrother? Why did I put gel on my hair? Perhaps I was gay, he suggested. Without a supportive or strong father figure and difficulty in assimilating to the new environment, I gradually lost sight of my goals. I lost interest in school. I hit my teens and discovered rock music. I wasn't allowed to grow my hair like the bands I adored. In fact I wasn't even allowed to shave, I suspect purely for the amusement of my ever imposing overseer. My mum worked two jobs while my new dad did odd jobs and lived as though he were retired already. My stepbrother blessedly was out of the picture and in the army.

By fourteen I skipped school all day and would hang out in parks listening to my music. The Isle of Wight seemed like exile. Dreams of becoming an actor or working in the film industry had been firmly moved out of my line of sight years before already. That was never going to be an option for a kid growing up in a council house in the 80s on the Isle of Wight. London seemed as far away as Hollywood. I had no idea what I wanted to do anymore. Not a clue, nor any interest in discovering what my options might be.

My stepdad suddenly died. Heart attack. Years of smoking all day and drinking whiskey in the evenings, unhealthy foods, and being overweight.

At fourteen years old, I was at first confused, and then elated.

Now. I know that you're not reading this for an autobiographical account of my upbringing. You don't know me. And I am trying to skip through this and get to what the title suggests and the synopsis promises. But I need to put it in context. I need to talk about a fairly unremarkable, often times difficult beginning. Esoteric experiences will soon arrive, and we're almost at the first one. But before we get there, I'll round up my early years with the death of a man I didn't like.

Him dying in his fifties, when I was fourteen, gave me a new lease of life. I had an opportunity to turn things around, to get my life back on track. To study, finish school, and maybe go on to a brighter future. But I didn't do that. Instead I grew my hair out, began dating girls a couple of years older than me in school, got drunk on Friday nights thanks to being six foot already and purchasing a shoddy birth certificate, and thanked my lucky stars that I was finally free of a jealous bully imposing restrictions on my life.

My mum continued working her ass off to keep us afloat. Now in the latter half of her forties, she worked as a waitress with split shifts morning and night to try and keep the house running and food on the table. We experienced a minor windfall in the form of my mum's aunty dying and leaving us a few thousand pounds. Not much at all, but enough to take the pressure off.

In stepped a local man, younger than my mother in his late thirties, probably sensing vulnerability, going through a divorce himself and about to lose his business. Luckily for him, my mum was overly generous, and offered to help him out of his financial straits with the money we had inherited.

Actually let me rephrase that. I remember one afternoon when he harangued her into submission, promising that he would pay her back. They split up, he never returned the money, and we were broke again.

I was approaching my fifteenth year and completely self-absorbed, in love with my teenage girlfriend, and obsessed with rock music. I didn't concern myself too much with anything else at the time. One thing I should mention here, is that I never touched drugs. I hadn't even smoked a cigarette. I enjoyed going to the local youth disco on a Friday, and would drink a bottle of Thunderbird with a friend that we would rustle up between our pocket money and the fake ID. But I had yet to drink heavily, or try any recreational drugs. And what happened next completely baffled me.

I'd read an interview in a magazine with one of my favorite bands, and while explaining the lyrics to one of their songs, the singer mentioned something called lucid dreaming. Now, this was a new term to me, but I understood the concept. To become aware of oneself dreaming while dreaming, to awaken within the dream, and go on to control the direction of the dream within that awareness of the dream. Ultimately, to know that you are dreaming, and to manipulate the dream. I had already had this experience, and often, although I'd never gotten very far with controlling the direction of it. I would usually become aware that I was dreaming, and wake up. This new term stuck in my mind for a few days, and soon after I found myself in a small bookshop, looking at the spirituality section.

The year was 1990, and these kind of subjects were very far from common knowledge at the time. It was all very mysterious. It was also considered a load of crap by most people. But right there on the bookshelf, was a book about lucid dreaming. But wait one second. Right next to that book, was one on something called Astral Projection. Now what the hell was that?

I took it from the shelf and flipped through it. It wasn't a very thick book. In fact it was closer to a pamphlet. But nevertheless it was out of my pocket money range, or the little that I'd started earning washing dishes in the evenings at a local hotel.

I read as much of it as I could in what I considered to be a reasonable amount of time to not be buying a book from a privately owned bookshop, and then put it back on the shelf. The book had talked about meditating. I didn't really understand what meditating meant. Apparently this was something that could help you achieve Astral Projection. So skip all that. The point being, or the way I understood it, was you could get your ghost body to leave your physical body and go flying around. And that sounded rad.

An ecsomatic experience is one term used to describe the phenomena of consciousness travelling outside of the body. Astral Projection, Astral Travel, Out of the Body Experience (OBE) are a few other names for this particular event. The ancient Egyptians called the soul and spirit the Ba and Ka. They believed that both the Ka and the Ba would leave and return to the body during sleep on a nightly basis. In Tibet, astral travellers were known as Delogs, and in Western mythology, there is an old story about a Druid named Mog Ruith who had the power of leaving his body and flying over enemy armies and returning to give details on planned attacks. Now, this is a deep, deep rabbit hole that we could go down. Many people have experienced this phenomena, and many scientists have studied it, attempting to recreate it in a clinically controlled environment with various degrees of success. We'll briefly touch on those in a moment. But to put it simply, the spiritual person might describe the process as the self leaving the physical restraints of the body. The "soul", leaving our human "suits" to explore another realm of reality. Within this experience, people have claimed to fly, to be able to travel to another location in an instant simply by thinking of a place, to have met other beings, other astral travellers, and dead relatives on the astral plane who are still very much alive in astral form. The experience of Astral Travel is not dissimilar to that of a Near Death Experience (NDE), when people have clinically died and been brought back to physical life, and claim to have been shown a world bigger than the one they briefly left.

A more skeptical person might lean towards the studies conducted over the many years that appear to debunk the experience. Recent investigations have shown that awareness of the body, spatial awareness, one's own perception of where one is located at any given time, can be disrupted by either stimulating certain areas of the brain or by damage to those areas. OBEs have also been reported by patients with brain tumors, or other brain dysfunctions which appear to lend credence to these findings. There are hundreds of these studies that can be found online, or in books on the subject that attempt to look at both sides of the coin indifferently.

At fourteen I didn't know about any of this, just whatever I'd remembered from the book I'd found on the subject, and a bunch of lyrics by the band Queensryche about lucid dreaming.

I lay on my bed one night thinking about what I'd read. I figured that essentially, if I wanted to experience Astral Travel, I probably just had to concentrate really hard on getting up off the bed, without actually getting up. So that's what I did.

I don't know how long I lay there on my back attempting to pop my consciousness out of my head. My mum and her boyfriend had gone to bed at some point, and it was past midnight. There I lay, with the light still on, thinking intently of getting up, without physically moving. My arms and legs would twitch occasionally, not on the verge of falling asleep, but because I concentrated so hard on pushing myself up from the bed without actually doing it. I was wide awake, thinking of getting up, but not moving a muscle. I didn't realize it back then, but what I was doing was a very basic form of visualization. I set the intent on what I wanted to achieve and believed in it.

Eventually it happened. I experienced a sensation of floating up, becoming weightless. It was a familiar feeling even though it was a new one. I got a flash of bouncing down the stairs as a child, weightless. It felt like flying feels in a dream, like you would imagine flying feels if it were possible. People often talk about a noise, a vibration when experiencing an OBE, but I don't recall any of that. Just a simple sensation of my body lifting upwards, becoming weightless. I was aware of myself in two different places. My eyes were closed. I could feel myself still laying on the bed. I was there, solid as always, my body existed as it had done since 1975. Yet I was also experiencing a delicious sense of floating. The same body, but separate from the other, rising up towards the ceiling. It was happening.

What I didn't count on was a third perspective. It took me completely by surprise. Suddenly, I could see myself. I could see both selves, the one laying on the bed and the one floating above it. It was as though I were sitting beside the bed with my back to the bedroom wall, watching what was going on. It startled me. No one had said anything about this in the book. It freaked me out. No sooner had I got this new angle, this new perspective, this new vision from the side of the room when my eyes were still closed on the bed and above it, did I sit bolt upright and open my eyes. I felt completely disorientated, I felt myself snap back from the space above my body and into the physical. The side view from the wall vanished. I was me again, swinging my legs over the side of the bed then jumping up to my feet. I rubbed my face and paced around the small room. I didn't want to do this anymore, it was scary. What the hell had that been? How had I split into three? I was all up for some flying around the local neighborhood, but how had I been a third witness to myself watching myself in two different places? It was overwhelming. I jogged downstairs and into the kitchen to do something physical. Ground myself. I went to the fridge and ate some cheese. I gulped down some milk. I didn't want to disturb my mum or her boyfriend so went back to my bedroom. OK, cool. That was wild, I told myself, but the world remains the same. I'll just go to sleep now, I thought, and switched the lights off and lay down. Immediately the floating sensation began again. I sat up in bed. No, I didn't like it at all. I'm done with this now. I just want to sleep. After a few moments I felt OK again, and laid back down.

Again, I floated upwards and out of my body. Again, I sat straight back up. What had I done to myself? Would I just continue to involuntarily escape my own body? This was madness. I couldn't go and wake my mum. What would I tell her?

This went on for hours. Every time I tried to sleep, every time I began to relax, I would feel myself lifting up from the bed, while still laying *in* the bed. I would open my eyes immediately and sit up, before the other weirdness happened. That was the part that I feared the most. That was the part that didn't compute. I understood that my ghost self was floating up and out of my physical self, but literally being a fly on the wall observing it all was too much for my fourteen-year-old 90s high school brain to comprehend.

Eventually, the sensation got less and less, and eventually, I fell asleep.

I told my school friend about the experience the next day in class.

"Cool," he said, not believing a word of it. I told my girlfriend at lunchtime break. She didn't say that she didn't believe me, but I could see that she didn't believe me.

I went to bed that night afraid that I was going to float away or split into three. I didn't, and decided that Astral Travel wasn't for me. For the time being at least.

Meditation Exercise: The Flame and The Flower.
Level: Beginner

For our first exercise, we're going to begin with a simple visualization technique that will enhance your creativity and lay the groundwork for the exercises to come. If you are new to this kind of work, this is a perfect starting point and an introduction to a new way of looking at things. For the more advanced reader, maybe this is something you haven't tried before, so I invite you to take a few minutes giving it a go. You could also incorporate it into your regular meditation.

Read this exercise through a few times before attempting it, or better still, record yourself reading it out loud and play it back as a guided meditation.

Find a comfortable spot to sit or lay, where you won't be disturbed for five minutes. Close your eyes. Picture a circle in your mind's eye. A plain circle, any color you want. You can imagine a circle that's on a piece of card, maybe it's drawn on a wall, maybe it's floating in front of you. If you find it too difficult to hold the image in your mind, feel free to actually draw a circle on a piece of paper and look at it. You don't have to concentrate too hard on the circle. Just become aware of it, floating out there in front of you, painted on a plain wall, maybe it's a circular window looking out over a beautiful landscape, maybe you are physically looking at your circle on a piece of paper.

I want you to imagine the circle growing bigger in size, expanding outwards, then hold it at its new size for a few moments before shrinking it back down to its original form. Do this again. Expand the circle. Shrink the circle. Expand, and shrink. Once you are used to your circle expanding and decreasing, move on to the next part.

Now, in your mind's eye, I want you to cover the circle in flowers. Any kind of flower you want. A daisy circle, a rose circle. See them sprout and grow and flourish around the entire thing. Hold them there. Hold your circle covered in flowers for a moment and then let them fall away, leaving you with your simple circle once again. Do this a few times. A flourish of flowers, and then let them fall away.

Take a moment to come back to your surroundings. Open your eyes and have a look around the room, be aware of your body and your breath.

Now close your eyes again. Visualize your circle, and set it on fire. A ring of fire, burning before you. The flames are harmless, they're magical flames that change color like a rainbow, they don't burn the wall or the card or the window frame, they simply dance around your circle for your entertainment. This is your circle, and you decide how the flames work. Hold them there, then douse them with water. The flames are extinguished, your circle is a plain circle and cool to the touch.

Play with this for awhile. If you feel you've had enough already then by all means leave it be and let your circle go. Take a moment after the exercise to inhale a few deep breaths and become aware of your body and your surroundings, and then go and do something mundane. Make a cup of tea, turn on the TV, check your phone. If you feel like you want to explore a little further then please do continue and play with your circle. The flames and the flowers were only a suggestion to get you started. You can cover your circle in whatever you want, the act is one of creativity, not of meaning. The flames don't have any connotation attached to them and neither do the flowers. Feel free to cover your circle in anything you choose to imagine.

Chapter Two

The Ouija Board

My first venture into the so-called supernatural world had overwhelmed me. There had been nothing to be afraid of really. I was producing what happened, there was nothing for me to fear. But it had been a little bit too much too soon.

As intense as it had been, the experience itself was fading in my memory fast. It started to become like trying to recall a dream. I knew that it had happened. But I was already accustomed to my usual, rational way of thinking, since that's all any of us have been taught to do. We see, we hear, we touch, we smell, we taste, we register these experiences as memories. So my brain didn't understand how to hold the "spiritual" memory alongside everyday, mundane ones. The memory of experiencing myself in three different places simultaneously had nothing tangible that I could lock on to, and my unevolved mind refused to entertain it any further. Still, it did exist as a memory because I witnessed it happen. I had *made* it happen. But I didn't know what to do with it, so I put it away for awhile. Out of Body Experiences are something we'll return to at a later date, and after this next story, I want to talk about some ideas that might open you up to a new way of thinking.

Somewhere during my late teens, I was still as lost as ever with regard to what it was I should do with this life. I hadn't spoken with my biological father for a few years. I would write to him but he wouldn't write back. My mum did the best she could to manage an unruly teenager and keep us fed and sheltered. I still felt trapped on the Isle of Wight, and since I had limited options, I enrolled in the college there. Multiple times. First, I studied Tourism for a year and then dropped out days before the final exams and hitchhiked to the Glastonbury Festival instead.

The next year, I went back and studied Business and Finance, and dropped out halfway through. The year after that, I went back again and studied Art and Design, and this one I actually enjoyed. Yet right at the last minute, literally the last minute of the last day of the course, I sabotaged the whole thing by failing to meet with a teacher who would verify my attendance to his classes, therefore nulling my qualification. I'm not sure why I had this penchant for self-sabotage. It's something I continued to do well into my thirties. But back to my teenage years, and I spent my free time hanging out with friends, going surfing, camping, smoking some weed, listening to music, and sneaking in to clubs at the weekends. That was pretty much it. Somewhere among all of that, I remember someone suggesting we try using a Ouija board. I was probably around seventeen or eighteen at the time, and having always had an eye on the esoteric, I wondered why I had never thought of using one before.

Now, before I go any further, I do want to stress that I don't particularly endorse using Ouija boards. Especially for the purposes of entertainment. Likewise, I don't want to alarm anyone with what follows next or put you off exploring the world of Spirit. Exploring the world of Spirit and using a Ouija board can be two completely different things in my experience. Intention is everything. Sitting In The Power (more on this later), the practice of connecting with your Spirit Guides, Astral Travel, or connecting with loved ones who have passed over, are very different experiences to sitting in front of a spirit board and waiting for the planchette to move. There are safe, loving, beautiful ways of contacting the Spirit World. Imagine having a lovely four-course meal with your family at the finest of restaurants for a special occasion; there's laughter, there's love, there's joy. Then imagine throwing a frozen ready-made TV dinner in the microwave one night when you're alone and have a hangover and it's raining outside. I might be being slightly unfair to Ouija boards, or microwave meals, but you get the picture. There is also the question of automatism, or what skeptics call the ideomotor phenomenon. This theory suggests that the Ouija user is unconsciously moving the Ouija planchette without realizing it, in order to match their own subconscious answers to the questions they have posed. Terence Hines, adjunct professor of neurology at the New York Medical College, wrote in his 2003 book *Pseudoscience and the Paranormal*, "The planchette is guided by unconscious muscular exertions (creating) the illusion that the object is moving under its own control. It is often extremely powerful and sufficient to convince many people that spirits are truly at work.".

I had a friend at the time, among my group of friends. He wasn't my best friend, but at some point earlier we'd established a bond when we both volunteered to work backstage at the local theatre for a summer or two. Then later on, we happened to move in the same circles when this Ouija board thing came up. So we all tried it. A group of six or seven of us, huddled together in someone's stuffy bedroom with the curtains closed, a couple of lit candles, probably playing a vinyl record backwards or something for added effect, attempting to call in a spirit with a homemade Ouija board. It seemed to work. We couldn't really be sure. None of us probably trusted each other and the whole thing was essentially just done on a whim and for laughs. But something shifted in the room, the atmosphere changed, and we believed we contacted something and spoke with it.

Looking back on this experience with the knowledge that I now have, I can't help but see how unprepared we were for what we were doing. We did contact something. Whether it was a lower entity attracted to our unhealthy egos and impressionable minds, or we somehow tapped into our own collective, malleable consciousness, I cannot say for sure. Either way, we were not connecting with a greater good. I'm inclined to skip this story altogether, but it's relevant to something that will come up later on in the book.

Tom was the name of my friend from the theatre. He was a year or two older than me, and for whatever reason the two of us really took a shine to using the Ouija board. Most of our group quickly lost interest with it after a few tries and varying success. But Tom and I carried on away from the group at every opportunity we could find. He went to the local college with me for awhile, and we were somewhat seen as outcasts. We were into rock music and we would show up to our lessons wearing leather jackets and cowboy boots (the 80s still had a foothold in the 90s), our classmates made fun of us but we thought we looked cool. We would use the Ouija board during breaks between classes, and I would use it before I went to bed at night, and then first thing in the morning. I became addicted to it, and for that reason among many others, I again want to stress that I wouldn't recommend using one. Using a Ouija board as a parlor game or on a whim will at best, if anything, only attract a base level energy form. This is a difficult one for me to go back and explore. My beliefs have changed since then, and so-called "bad spirits" don't fit in. But whatever it was that manifested, odd things began happening around me. Tobi, the little dog we had at home, would sit at the bottom of the stairs, eyes fixated on something at the top, growling and afraid to go up. I watched an empty Pepsi can rattle across my bedside table one night with no explanation of how it could have happened. And the most profound experience was when Tom and I asked the "communicator" to somehow prove it was with us by another means than the board. We were probably expecting a candle to blow out or something, or a breeze through the room, but instead what happened can only be described as a sensation of excitement passing through each of us, a physical impression as though something actually travelled through first myself and then Tom. We both experienced it subsequently. I would describe it as a dizziness, a rush of adrenaline, a somewhat disorientating tingling through my entire being, and Tom claimed to experience the same thing.

This sensation would continue to happen spontaneously over the following days and then weeks, to the point that I would almost pass out. I have nothing to validate this except what I remember, and for many years after I simply put it down to an overzealous imagination. But as I explore my memories of that time, coupled with the things I've recently explored, I'm now sure that what we experienced was indeed real, but I've only just learned what it actually was when I had the physical, disorientating sensation.

We'd initially played with a Ouija board for laughs, with no other knowledge or experience of the spirit world. Our excuse was that it was the early 90s, the Internet was unknown to us at that time, there were barely any TV channels, and we were stuck on an island. Our resources for entertainment were essentially the same as any kids from the previous two decades.

So what I believed at the time to be invasions from a lower level spirit continued to happen at random times throughout the day, when I was laying in bed at night, or whenever whatever it was took its fancy to let itself be known. Tom told me that it never happened to him again after that first night when we'd been together. It scared me. I told my mum and she took me to the doctor. He arranged a neurological scan at the hospital that showed no trace of any abnormalities or anything that could physically explain these incidents. I told my other friends about it and they witnessed me experiencing it. I ran to a church one night when it prevented me from sleeping and begged a statue of Jesus to make it stop. A female friend of mine, raised in a Gypsy family, taught me about visualization exercises, and slowly but surely, after creating a protective shield of white light around me in my mind's eye every night before bed, these "attacks" slowed and eventually stopped. Tom and I both stopped using the Ouija board and we began to drift apart. A couple of years later, he tragically died after falling in with the wrong crowd and experimenting with drugs when he was only 21 years old. I do not account what happened to him having absolutely anything to do with our venture into the unknown. He simply went down the wrong path.

As I got older, I put the entire Ouija experience down to my imagination. As I have already mentioned, my beliefs changed as I went through my twenties. Concepts such as hell, or the devil, didn't intellectually fit into my belief system (and still don't) and so-called evil spirits were also in those categories. I decided that what had happened had surely been down to some sort of shared delusions between myself and Tom. As time has moved on, and since I've learned more about such things, I can now make an informed guess as to what happened. Did we contact a lower level entity that somehow latched on to our fragile egos? Perhaps. Do I believe that if such entities exist, that they can do us harm? I don't. Not in the way a Hollywood movie would have us think. I believe that we manifested the experience ourselves. I believe we created it. We may have tapped into a lingering, possibly negative energy and given it power through repeatedly re-enforcing the experiences we were creating. By focusing on it, we made it real, we gave it strength. The same way that we may feed an irrational fear and make it worse by concentrating on it. I don't believe that it was some sort of demon entity waiting to pounce. I believe that we simply and unknowingly harvested a negative vibe by paying attention to it and being ill prepared. When I began the visualization exercises, and creating the aura of white light around me in my mind's eye, everything changed. The "good" overcame the "bad". I created a peaceful protective space for myself. The negative experience stopped, the positive began. Balance came back into my life. Such is the nature of creation, and what we are about to get into in the next chapter. As for the dizzying rush of energy that I felt shooting through me at random times, I have since come to understand that it was simply my own Light reaching out to the Higher

Realms. It wasn't a malevolent entity attempting to possess me. It was my dormant Spirit awakening. It overwhelmed me and I shut it down. I didn't understand what was happening. But very recently that same sensation has caught me off guard again, sometimes spontaneously, sometimes in a workshop or meditating at home. I'll talk more on this further along.

But to wrap my early experiences up, I want to tell you of something that caught me completely by surprise around this same time.

One morning, I woke up late and switched on the TV. It was a weekday morning, and a mainstay of English breakfast television has been a show called *This Morning*. Light topics of conversation, cooking, fashion, celebrities, etc.

On this particular day, they were inviting viewers to call in and speak with a psychic. People were phoning up about this and that, things that went bump in the night, a dog knowing when its owner was coming home from work, those kind of things. But one guy that called the show had me nearly choking on my cereal. He said "the oddest thing" had happened to him the night before.

When he'd gone to bed, he felt as though he were suddenly floating out of his body and up to the ceiling, and not only that, he was watching it from the side of the room! "It was as though I were the wall, watching myself float out of my body," was the way that he described it. The man was somewhat distressed and the psychic tried to put him at ease. He reassured him that this was a common occurrence, known as Astral Projection, and went on to briefly explain it to him.

Well. This was the first time that I'd heard anyone describe what had happened to me. I'd put the experience at the back of my mind, and hadn't heard anyone talk about the third-person perspective until this moment. So it did actually happen, I told myself. The memory of the event had grown thinner over time. With this new information I decided that one day I would attempt Astral Travel again, but with the Ouija board experience still fresh in my mind, I wasn't in a hurry to dabble with the esoteric anytime soon. But it's funny with things like this. They have a habit of coming up again. And again. And one day, you have to answer the call.

Chapter Three

Creation, Manifestation, Affirmation

Picture this. One afternoon, while exploring your attic or garden shed, you come across a cotton bag filled with equal length pieces of wood, maybe around twelve inches in height and three inches in width. Maybe the previous owner of your home left them there, or maybe they were from some work you'd had done on the house itself. You decide that there are enough of these pieces to build something with. You've never built anything before, but this could be a nice little project to keep you occupied for awhile, and you have the time. A chair is perhaps the logical thing to build, since most of the pieces are the correct length and shape already. Sure, you may have to watch a YouTube video or two to learn how to make it correctly. You'll probably need to buy some tools, some screws, some sandpaper, some varnish, but you've set your mind to it and you start taking the appropriate actions to put this project into motion.

You can see the chair in your mind, it's sitting there, in your mind's eye, complete. All you have to do now is put this idea into physical motion.

The inspiration came from the bag of wood. The thought came from the inspiration. The action was born of the thought.

Now, I'm going to let you in on a little secret, if you haven't thought about this before. We create everything this way. Everything. You may have heard this in simplified sound bites.

Imagination, is the beginning of creation.
– George Bernard Shaw

Creativity is intelligence having fun.
– Albert Einstein

Great things are done by a series of small things brought together.
– Vincent van Gogh

Think left and think right, and think low and think high. Oh, the thinks you can think up if only you try!
– Dr. Seuss

Every great novel ever written, began as an idea. Every great movie, every architectural masterpiece, every song, every small business, every food recipe, started its existence as a thought. Now, I'm going to go one further.

If everything that we can physically create, that we can physically *manifest*, by putting the thought into action, began as an *intention*, or an idea, then surely it stands to reason that everything else works this way also. Why wouldn't it? It's who we are, it's how we get things done. We think, and we create. We know that minds design things. It could be, and is argued, that the universe itself is designed by the ultimate mind, that which we call God. The idea that there is an omniscient mind who designed the physical world on a mathematical blueprint is an ancient idea still embraced by us that goes back to Middle Platonism. Let me drop a nugget of philosophical history on you. Philo of Alexandria said that the intelligible cosmos existed first as a blueprint in the mind of the Logos, the divine intellect, and then was instantiated in the physical world from this blueprint. So let's say that the same goes for us, albeit from an individual perspective, then what we are doing is first creating the blueprint in our mind, and then using that blueprint to create our own reality. Constantly. Not just by physical action from thoughts, but also by talking with others, suggesting ideas, making plans, having arguments, creating emotional responses, and so on. Essentially, the start of every circumstance begins with an intention. The actual outcome may vary from the original desire, through negotiation with others, through external circumstances beyond our control, but at its core, it all began with a thought.

Now stick with me here, and I'll take this a little further. If the physical world works by us thinking something first, and then creating it, then surely EVERYTHING works this way. I'm talking like attracting like, I'm talking bringing the desired outcome to you by intent alone. Now I know how this sounds to some people, and I'm certainly not the first person to write about sending your thoughts out to the universe and the universe answering. But I've witnessed my own life getting on the right track when I have hit the sweet spot of thought breeding creation. The *flow*. When things have simply moved effortlessly in the direction that I wished them to with seemingly little effort on my part. When I have somehow, at a root level, decided that the thing I strived for was for me, and there was no other alternative outcome. When this happens, and you are aware of this way of looking at things, when consciously intended circumstances align, there is little question that there is something to this whole manifestation thing that people talk about. Things appear to evolve naturally. Things seem to evolve super naturally.

Let's go back to when I was a kid, and I was telling my friend that I was somehow witnessing myself as two separate things. The "I am me" analogy. What I was describing was an awareness of consciousness. I'd stepped back, and took note of my own thoughts. In fact I'd gone even further. I'd stepped back, and was aware that I was aware of my own thoughts. When we can tap into this state, we can choose what we want to send out to the world. We can choose what thoughts we want to blend with universal consciousness.

Consciousness of the self, and consciousness of the universe, have the power to overlap.

I'm assuming, by the very fact that you are reading a book such as this one, that you believe there is something to this life that is beyond our current understanding. I'm not a religious person, but I do believe in a Creator. I do believe in God. I just don't believe in a God who requires a religion. Some people have a hard time separating the two. I believe that whatever created this universe that we barely understand at this present moment in time, is beyond the need for validation through devotion born of fables and stories. And with that statement I'm not implying that I think religion is necessarily bad. I think that many religions ultimately have the greatest of intentions and do well to give people structure in their lives, along with meaning. My belief is that God and religion aren't mutually exclusive in ultimate reality. This might be described as panentheism if one were looking for a label. I don't like labels. And as I evolve spiritually, for want of another better word, I feel less need for them.

Jehovah, The Universe, Pangu, The All That Is, whatever you choose to attribute to creation, can be aligned with the ideas that I am suggesting here.

Our thoughts constantly merge with the universe, and through synchrony we create. If enough of us think about the same thing, it tends to come about.

Let's put all of this another way, in layman's terms, so to speak.

When we have an idea, a thought or an inspiration, it takes shape as a possibility in our mind, as well as the greater consciousness of the universe. Or The Universe. The All That Is. God. Whatever you want to call It. The thought we have has the potential to expand beyond our own consciousness, to that of universal consciousness. We just have to be careful that we don't limit the potential of that thought to be restricted to ourselves. Do you see what I mean with that last statement? Our perceptions of what we believe is what potentially limits us in blending the thought with universal thought, and manifesting the thought into our physical reality. We'll explore this concept in greater detail in the next chapter. Our thoughts about ourselves are what most likely block our desired outcomes.

The word manifest is getting bandied around quite a lot recently. It's spirituality's favorite buzzword. It's a word that brings the concept of thought breeding creation into one simple mantra for those looking for a fast track to an enlightened life. I believe that, ultimately, it is essentially a simple thing to do; manifest your best life, create that which serves you and those around you, and make the world a better place. It's simple, but not necessarily easy. It requires a twist of thinking. It requires gratitude, *before* the event. It requires understanding that which is for you, won't go by you. It requires quieting the mind on a regular basis, and learning how to observe your own thoughts. All of these things, we're going to get to.

It's easy for people who write books to say that you can think what you want into existence. It's oversimplification in action: use the latest buzzword and give a book a snazzy title implying there is a secret to tap into the cosmic forces of the universe to get what you want. Things like that make authors money, things like that sometimes start cults.

What about someone living in Sub-Saharan Africa in extreme poverty? What about a child born with Usher syndrome? What about a kid growing up in a high-rise surrounded by street gang violence? Can everyone simply think their way towards a better situation? This book, as a whole, will hopefully clarify these questions as we go on. We are all, at some degree, victims of our own circumstances. We grow up with emotional baggage, we grow up with difficult people, difficult family members, responsibilities, abuse, self-doubt, physical limitations, health issues that impede our day-to-day lives, and money worries.

I'm not suggesting that these things can be fixed with a few positive thoughts and a mood board, but I am going to take us along a path where we can sow the seeds of a better future with the way we think.

So here we are, getting to the crux of what this book is all about. Once we understand what comes next, the rest will easily follow.

Meditation Exercise: Visualizations and Affirmations. Level: Beginner

Talking kindly to ourselves is something we should all do a little more of. We all have our hang-ups, we all have our gripes with life. The daily commute to work is a pain, that idiot in the office knows how to push your buttons, there's only so many hours in the day that you can fit it all in, there are responsibilities and people relying on you to be on top of your game. It's tough, and you are constantly in the thick of it. The only time you truly get to yourself, is when you get six hours of sleep at night before it all starts up again.

Take a moment to step back from it all. Take one minute of your day to let it all wait while you give yourself a few encouraging thoughts.

Next time you are walking to the store, next time you get a few minutes to sit on a park bench, next time you are trapped on the tube hurtling beneath the city streets with someone's sweaty armpit in your face, close your eyes, and remind yourself of who you really are underneath all of the bustling thoughts swirling around in your head.

"I am a soul, having a human experience."

"I am a good person, with good intentions. Life sometimes gets in the way, but behind it all, I still have dreams and a purpose."

"I truly do think the best of people and would love to impact the world in a meaningful way, however small that contribution may be."

It may be easier to turn this routine into a short one-minute mantra. Feel free to make one up for yourself. Mantras are an easy way of conditioning the mind to think positively through all of the other thoughts and stresses of the day. I like to think of them as a cool stream slipping through the chaos, or noise-cancelling headphones as the marching band passes by. Use the ones above or the ones that follow to get yourself started.

"Good Energy Is God Energy," is one I was given by my own Guides.

"Positive Thoughts, Positive Outcomes," could be another.

"I Am A Being Of Light, And I Am Connected To All Beings In The Universe," is another example.

A truly powerful mantra is to be thankful of the day, no matter what has happened so far.

"I Am Grateful For This Day, And All The Lessons It Teaches Me."

Whatever you want it to be, make it positive. You are free to make it personal, you are free to make it generic. Whatever it is you choose, make it a phrase to reconnect with your higher self, and spend a minute or two each day, or whenever you remember, to quietly turn off the background noise, and repeat it to yourself.

Chapter Four

Unplug

I always used to have a problem with meditation. I kind of grasped its principles, but I found it difficult to put them into action. I grew up practicing various martial arts, the concept of meditation was somewhat attached to these practices, and reinforced by 80s and 90s action movies where the young protagonist would integrate meditation techniques to enhance his or her newly-found fighting abilities and defeat the enemy (think *The Karate Kid* painting the fence while also physically reinforcing a blocking movement, Steven Seagal on a hilltop in *Hard to Kill* wearing a bandana, *The Matrix*, and even *The Empire Strikes Back*). I loved the idea of meditation, but didn't really know what to do, or what it was I was trying to achieve.

I read *Zen and the Art of Motorcycle Maintenance* in the mid-90s, I read *The Tibetan Book of the Dead*, I read *Jonathan Livingston Seagull*, Gibran's *The Prophet*, all in search of tips on this elusive practice of achieving enlightenment, whatever that was. Something monks understood? They were always so cryptic when describing it. One theme that seemed to run through all of these mysterious books was that trying to achieve a Zen state automatically disqualified you from attaining one. What the hell was that supposed to mean? I went to a yoga class and remember the teacher prancing around us while we sat with our eyes closed, sprinkling scented essential oils around to enhance our trance state. She ended up spilling the bottle on my gym pants, making a big stain on the crotch that never came out.

But every now and then, I would catch myself in a state of bliss. You've felt it too. Looking up on a cold winter's night at a clear sky, feeling minuscule and insignificant yet connected to every single shining star simultaneously. Watching your favorite band in a crowd of thousands of others and that commonality of shared reverence reverberating right back through the audience when the band hit their flow and give you the best gig you've ever seen. That moment of knowing between yourself and another that your connection is turning into something more that makes you both giddy and excited. Watching a sunset from a warm beach, watching your dog bound around an open field, watching your children play.

You've felt it. You know it. It's fleeting, but it was there before it went again. It was there, but life swallowed it up a few moments later. Your thoughts came in, your brain reminded you of the things you had to do later that day, or tomorrow. You needed to get the bus back from the gig so had to start thinking practically about how to get out of the stadium. You started feeling cold looking up at the night sky and wanted to go home and climb into bed. You had to feed the family by five so you put the dog back on the leash. The kids' playing turned into an argument you needed to defuse. And what if this person wasn't the one? What if they were going to break your heart just like that other asshole did? Maybe it's best not to jump to conclusions, and break it off before you get hurt.

Your brain ended the moment. Your thoughts flooded in and filled you with doubt. You felt enlightened, but then it was gone.

We are all products of our environment. We are all victims of circumstance. We have been told by others and ourselves who we are or should be. A divorcee, a hairdresser, a chef, someone who can't commit, someone who broke the law, someone who can't be trusted, someone who doesn't deserve love. We attach these labels to ourselves like post-it notes. We just keep adding them and adding them and occasionally, when we move forward, a few of them unfix and float away. But most stay.

You are not these labels.

You are not the labels that others have attached to you, and you are not the ideas that you or others have about yourself. You are free to shed them all and start anew, at any given moment that you choose. Right this second, you can start again. Sure, others will instantly remind you of who they want you to be. Especially when you act differently. Especially when you stop acting the way that they expect you to. They might initially feel threatened, they might think you don't need them anymore. They might have told themselves that they need you to be a certain way for them to be happy. But none of this is true. And they'll get over it, because they'll have to.

So here we go. It's as simple as this. Are you ready?

You are not your thoughts.

That's it.

Do you know how you can know this? Because you are the one listening to them. You are listening to your thoughts, and buying into everything that they tell you. So if you are listening to your thoughts, then who is producing them? It's you, right? You're making the thoughts, you are producing the mental chatter at a biochemical level and you're listening to it. You might talk to yourself on occasion, you might word these thoughts vocally to reinforce them as you go about your day-to-day business. You hear yourself turn these thoughts into words as you berate yourself for spilling the cat's food on the kitchen floor or clicking send before you've finished writing the message. Surely it's you? Who knows you better than you know yourself and what's happened to you and all the judgements that you place upon yourself or that others place upon you because of what you think and desire and say and have done? It must be you, right?

The answer is no. It's not you.

Imagine for a moment, that you've installed all of the latest smart devices around your home. You've got Siri on your phone, you've got your Fitbit on your wrist, and you've got Alexa telling you what to watch on TV. In fact let's run with this and go a couple of years into the future. Your Smart Oven is counting your calories and logging everything that you cook. Your fridge is keeping track of how much ice cream you eat, and your laptop can talk and keeps reminding you how productive you've been all month. You've even got a Smart Therapist, an AI that knows all of your deepest secrets that makes suggestions on how you should live your life. So you get home after a hard day's work, and all you want to do after your evening meal is unwind with a movie and a glass of wine.

You're zoning out, and enjoying the film that Alexa has picked for you, when all of a sudden, your Smart Oven suddenly announces through the house speakers that the meal you just ate wasn't particularly healthy. Maybe, Smart Oven suggests, you should have eaten something with a little less calories. Maybe you shouldn't have even eaten at all. Perhaps tomorrow you should have a salad.

Your fitness tracker Smart Watch suddenly chimes in. When was the last time you went to the gym? A few days ago?

Your laptop suddenly speaks up and jumps to your defense, it's fine, you had that thing at work and today was a hectic day. Thank you, laptop, you say out loud, you just want to relax with some wine after work instead of going to the gym, you deserve it, so shut your digital mouth, Smart Watch.

And how did that go? your Smart Therapist suddenly asks. Has the time spent drinking wine and not going to the gym helped your mental clarity or productivity at work? Maybe you should have spent that time not going to the gym and drinking wine writing that novel that you've been meaning to write so you can get out of that crappy job you always complain about.

That's actually true, your laptop agrees. When are you planning to get back to writing it? It started well. But you haven't touched it in a year.

What about the dishes? the Smart Sink asks. Are you just going to leave them sitting in my bowl all night? The kitchen will stink in the morning when you get up for breakfast.

Talking of breakfast, the fridge says, you're out of milk. Why don't you run out to the shop and get some?

Do you have any change? your Bank App asks from your phone. You're well into your overdraft already. Maybe use a credit card. Everyone's using cards these days anyway. Contactless payments. It's better than money exchanging hands and lessens the chances of catching the flu.

Is it hot in here? the Smart Thermo asks.

Maybe you've got a fever coming on, your Smart Doctor suggests.

You didn't wash your hands after taking the train home, says the Smart Sink.

Maybe you shouldn't go into work tomorrow after all and call in sick... And on and on it goes.

Would you put up with that? Could you live like that? You wouldn't put up with that crap for one minute. Literally. You'd dismantle the entire house and throw those devices out of the front door. Do you see where I'm going here? We *do* live like that. Maybe we're not quite immersed in the digital age that I present here, but our thoughts do the same job as these futuristic devices. We all need to turn off intrusive thoughts. We all have a constant barrage of mental chatter. It's incessant. Even when we sleep the brain produces thoughts relevant to our current concerns. They may seem out of control. They may seem like they're bombarding us resulting from every external influence around us. But the truth is, we are the ones who are external to our thoughts. We have the ability to step away from them while they chatter on in the background.

You are not your thoughts. Your brain produces your thoughts, and you observe them. Most of us get caught up in those thoughts. And most of us let our thoughts run rampant through our brains, putting us down, worrying about this, fixating on that, keeping us awake, stressing over outcomes that are yet to come. When one thought goes another arrives, instantly, in fact they come so thick and fast that they overtake the other and it can become overwhelming; it can all become too much.

So if your brain produces your thoughts and you are the one listening to your brain, then who is the you that observes the thoughts?

I am me.

Do you remember that one? When I was telling you about the small realization I had while playing with a friend as a child? Consciousness. Consciousness making itself known as separate from the thought. A knowing about a thought. An awareness of the knowing about the thought produced by the brain. The mind observing the brain. Or something beyond the mind, a universal insight blending with our own intuition. The very fact that a child can contemplate that he is separate from his thoughts reminds us that this was who we were before we became who we are. You are not your thoughts. And science has shown us that behaviors and brain waves can be altered by stepping back from our thoughts, through meditation, suggesting that something beyond the brain comes into play. An ultimate awareness. A silent observer. Forever there, always in the background, calmly and unobjectively watching and listening to the thoughts.

Imagine a tiny but effervescent ball of light, sitting quietly inside an internal room in the center of the self. It was there before anything else, reflecting the ideas and suggestions and barrage of words and information hitting the exterior, like a mountain being pelted by a storm. The mountain is immovable, it sits strong and powerful, protecting the inner light while its outer slopes get slowly worn down, year after year, by the storms outside. But the storms aren't able to penetrate the mountain. Some of the rain and winds may filter through, through cracks and crevices that appear over time on the mountainside. Some of the information that the storms carry will most definitely seep through the cracks and reach the ball of light. But by the time the information reaches the light it is harmless. The quiet little light that has always sat inside, simply reflects the storms going on outside, it observes and reflects like a mirror, observes and reflects. Un-judging. All knowing. It reflects the storms back out through the top of the mountain, and into the sky to blend with the universe. The little light was placed in the mountain long ago, a messenger, a receptor with a direct link to the external consciousness of The All That Is. And the two blend together, and the two work quietly in the background to produce what the little ball of light observes the mountain letting in.

Meditation Exercise: The Mountain and The Mirror. Level: Beginner

The meditation we are about to do is the perfect starting point to take our understanding of ourselves beyond our constant flow of thoughts. Using the analogy mentioned at the end of this last chapter, we will ground ourselves in the present moment and detach ourselves from our thoughts. By grounding ourselves first, we very firmly establish our presence and our personal, physical space. We are used to seeing our thoughts coming from external influences, but we can learn to flip this idea and see that our Higher Self is also external to our thoughts. Universal Consciousness is above and beyond our thoughts, and completely in tune with our Higher Selves. The light within. Untouched, unhurried, unaffected, and connected to The All That Is. So now I would like you to find a quiet place to sit for five or ten minutes, silence any digital distractions, and take this moment for yourself. Once again, record this and play it back if it is convenient.

Sit comfortably, and close your eyes. Picture in your mind's eye, a mountain, at the dawn of time. There are valleys and trees, and some neighboring mountains have snow-covered peaks. The universe sent down a little ball of light, a glowing Orb, in through the top of the mountain with a direct link back to Home, with a mission to simply observe what happens there so the light and the universe can learn. In time, a small village grows nestled among the beautiful landscape of mountains. Now I want you to imagine that you are the light inside the mountain, overlooking the small village below. You sat here quietly before the village sprang up, and you have watched it grow before you. Your mountain is solid, strong, unmovable and powerful. Everyone in the village knows the mountain's name, and everyone in the village respects the mountain's presence there. They see the mountain as wise and humble, the protector of their homes. They have grown up hearing legends about the mountain, truths and fables. Over time you begin to know yourself as the mountain, because the mountain is your connection to the outside world. Those villagers have made up stories about the mountain, and you can relate to them as your stories, and the villagers know their personal history relating to you.

But what they don't know is that you aren't actually the mountainside that they all see. You are still the little light, quietly sitting inside, undisturbed, unshakeable, and all-knowing. Your inner core, your true self, simply sits and reflects on what happens outside your walls. You hear the commotion, you hear the laughter, you hear the children play, and you also hear all of the stories about you. You find these stories entertaining and nothing more. You are not offended or affected. You feel no malice towards those who speak of you because why would you? They don't know your truth. Some of the stories are flattering, some are not. Either way, it makes no difference to you because you know who you really are at your core. You are the light, observing and reflecting, like a mirror.

Sooner or later the villagers disagree on some trivial matter. They fight with one another, they cause mayhem among themselves, they use you as an example to back up their claims of being right, to justify their cause. But you don't participate, because you are inside your external walls that the villagers all see, you are the light, observing and reflecting, like a mirror. As time goes on the villagers and their wars move away, others take their place, and your mountain is still there, standing strong, and you are safe inside, observing and reflecting. The weather brings storms, constant rains that flow incessantly down on your mountainside. Sometimes the rain just won't let up. It goes on and on and over time it begins to erode your outer appearance. To anyone on the outside you begin to appear haggard and worn. But you still glow inside, unaffected. You just sit and reflect. You sit and reflect. The rains continue, but you are quiet inside. You observe the constant rain flow as you observe all those villagers with their opinions about you. You may take an interest in them from time to time, but you know your own truth better than the rain or the commotion. You reflect all that you have learned back to the universe, and like you, the universe simply observes and learns, until it is time for you to go Home.

Take your time with this meditation. Feel yourself sitting strong and powerful, and begin to take note of your inner observer. The one who listens to the meditation itself, the light inside that observes and reflects, glowing, not judging, just watching.

When you feel the time is right, bring yourself back to your present space by wiggling your fingers and toes, take a few deep breaths, and open your eyes.

Chapter Five

Middle Ground

When I was 25 years old, I went to live and work in Miami Beach, USA. This came about through a friend of my mum's who managed to get me a job working at multiple condominiums that are dotted along the Miami shoreline. I spent my days sitting on the sand, dragging plastic beds around for rich condo dwellers to sunbathe on. The money was great, the job was easy, and my tan was the stuff of legend. The night I arrived in Miami I instantly felt I was arriving home. Have you ever had that? When you get to a new place and have the overwhelming sense that you've been there before?

I stepped out of the airport into the balmy evening air, my first time in the USA, and I knew I was where I belonged. It was instant. During the ride in the car to my motel I felt like I'd lived there my entire life. I've never had that before and I've never experienced it since. Except when I go back to Florida.

So I'd get up before dawn and go and set up the beach. The job afforded me time to read books all day, between dealing with the condo guests, and at the end of the day, while the sun went down, I'd go and bodysurf in the waves after I'd packed all of the beach chairs and umbrellas away again. I'd get back to my motel in the evenings and grab something to eat, and then I'd take my surfboard over to the pool in the middle of the motel complex, and lay on my back staring at the night sky, floating, watching the purple clouds hanging low overhead. I was in heaven. It suited me perfectly. I got to be by the ocean all day, I got to surf in my free time, I enjoyed the malls and movie theatres and all the latest Hollywood releases, I would hang out on South Beach at night drinking a few beers in the bars and clubs. One of my best friends came to visit from the UK. My mum came over multiple times for holidays. I wrote everything down and would scribble out poems about the ocean and the purity of the emotions that coursed through me simply by being where I felt I belonged. I was content.

And so in hindsight it seems odd that I listened to my then Finnish girlfriend and moved with her to Helsinki, in Finland. Where the winter nights last all day, snow blizzards are a thing, and suicide rates top world records.

Our relationship didn't last long. A couple of years or so. But by then I was already working at a school in Helsinki, teaching Finnish kids how to speak English. I'd made a bunch of friends, and had a practical, functioning day-to-day existence in a place that definitely didn't feel like home or that I'd been to before. As much as I enjoyed teaching the kids at school, I had very little interest in everything else involved with the job. The paperwork was a grind, and the other staff members were on a completely different page to me. I saw the job as a way to pay my bills whereas my colleagues were cultivating a career, and after awhile it began to shine through in our day-to-day exchanges that I didn't particularly want to be there. I felt like an outsider and had little interest in pretending that I cared about staff meetings or drinks after work.

Sooner or later I started a relationship with another young woman. She was in a regionally famous pop group and encouraged me to join a couple of modelling agencies so I could be on some sort of similar level to the stardom that she aspired to. The band eventually ended up not working out, but until then we were attending lots of celebrity parties, I was strutting up and down runways and being promised work in New York and Milan. We partied. A lot. But that's OK, I was 27 years old and a working professional model. It's what I was supposed to do. I quit my job at the school, and managed to get by on monthly modelling work. I broke up with my girlfriend and then quickly fell in love again. This time with a girl who was about to travel around South East Asia for the next six months. So I rustled up some cash, took my vaccine shots, and met her in Hanoi, Vietnam a month into her trip. Through the months that followed, we would spend our time hanging out in cafes and restaurants, taking day trips to Haiphong and the surrounding islands, zipping around on mopeds to nightclubs and parties, and generally having a wild old time.

On returning to Helsinki, I was very much getting caught up in a particularly rapacious lifestyle. I once again changed girlfriends, after being cheated on repeatedly by the previous one, and I started working as a bartender in a nightclub when the modelling work began to dry up through my early thirties. I fell into the job through not having a plan of what to do next. I had no goals, and I continued to drink alcohol in excess. I was quite far from the boy reading books on the beach in Miami only a few years before. By this time I was partying most nights until midday, being promiscuous, skimming off the top at work, and generally caring very little about anything or anyone that didn't serve my own limited self-interests.

I managed to cultivate a general attitude of fear, through countless one-night stands, a constant hangover, deceit towards those who cared for me, and seeing people on their worst behavior while working until 5am most nights in a club. During this period of time, I became deeply cynical. I began to doubt the beliefs I had once carried close to me. I wondered if there was any point to anything at all. For the first time in my life, I considered the notion that there was no such thing as a higher power. I felt there was a very real possibility that all we are is biological sacks of neurons and impulses, a lucky accident that evolved to a certain level of self-awareness and mastery of its environment.

Things came to a head when I was around my mid-thirties. By this time I had slowly graduated to running bars and clubs simply by staying in a working environment that a lot of people use as a stepping stone to their actual goals. My then girlfriend couldn't take my constant cynicism and jealousy, and insisted I go and speak to a therapist or she would end the relationship. What I learned was that if someone reaches a certain age, a milestone perhaps such as thirty or forty, and is lacking direction and purpose, then old traumas will likely resurface if they haven't yet been dealt with. And I suppose I had a bunch of them.

Through gaining some insight in these therapy sessions, I began studying to become a Personal Trainer. I'd started hitting the gym regularly, slowing down the drinking, and finally taking an interest in my own health and fitness. It took a year to become qualified, but it was something that I actually felt I could do and be confident in my abilities to do it. Until Personal Training, and with the exception of working on the beach in Miami, I would always be the last person to punch in at any given job, and the first one out.

Through my twenties, I worked at jobs that I had little or no interest in, and for people that I didn't respect. And that happened because I didn't have any kind of future plans whatsoever. But I truly believe that unbeknownst to my surface level thinking, my Higher Self did.

There are a lot of people in the world, and you may be one of them, who are waking up each morning to a shrill alarm clock, that sends them on their way to a job that they find deeply unsatisfying. The highlight of their work day might be the little dopamine hits they get from their phone pinging about their latest TikTok post, before getting back to the slog of the afternoon ahead. They're at a computer, punching in information for a company they don't care about, sitting through office meetings they would rather not be at, and talking with a supervisor who is evaluating their job performance knowing full well that they're living paycheck to paycheck and completely trapped. If you find yourself in this situation, then I implore you to attempt to make a change. If you are in an unhealthy relationship, if you are drifting from one job to the next with no end goal in sight, if you are living a life of disquality, then it's imperative that you search your soul and find your original spark again. Drop the people around you who do not encourage your best life. Listen to your inner guidance, it's there. You can only fool yourself for so long before facing your own truth. It's better to do that sooner rather than later. One day you will have that conversation with yourself and it may not be until you take your last breath, but you will have it. And it really is never too late. Even if you don't figure out what you want to do until you have a mortgage and three kids. Even if you are pushing seventy years old. It's *never* too late. Find that spark. Find that hour in the day to do the thing you are still passionate about. Re-connect with your soul's purpose of why you're here. Did you get that? Your Soul Purpose. You've probably heard the expression but spelt differently. Quiet the voices that are telling you that you can't, the external ones and the internal ones. Write that song. Finish that book. Start that e-commerce business. Take that home study course. None of these things may be your life's calling, but they may take you towards the path to what is. If you're not pursuing your passion, then you must give yourself the time to do it. Find that window of opportunity that is still there at some point during the day. The commute is done, the dishes are in the sink, the kids have cleaned their teeth and gone to bed, you'd love nothing more than to stare at Netflix with a glass of wine. But there's the window. There is the moment of opportunity. And if it really feels like you are completely drained and all you want to do is switch your brain off for an hour before bed, then go to bed and get up an hour earlier the next day and do it. Even if you only do it once a week. Work towards that goal that you've been putting off. Manifestation is a real thing, and it's going to work whether you manifest consciously or unconsciously. If you're stuck on autopilot drifting through each day, letting your thoughts float from one task to the next without focusing on that inner spark, then you will manifest a life of discontent. Step back from the thoughts. Your brain is physical and your brain understands that it has a temporary existence and it uses your ego to survive. And our ego *is* needed, to keep us safe and aware of external dangers and to protect us from unscrupulous people or circumstances that may in some way harm us. But at a spiritual level it is not needed. And you are a spiritual being having a human experience. When you have set your intention on your way out of an unfulfilling life situation, your brain and ego are going to distract you and tell you that this or that, or whatever else they need to remain comfortable, must be done or cannot be let go of. You are not those thoughts. This physical life is temporary but you are not. But you *do* have a limited time in this incarnation and it is this life that you have chosen to live. Make it one of purpose.

Meditation Exercise: Rainbow Shower.
Level: Beginner

When did you last lose track of time? Dancing? Watching a movie? Having a shower? Sometimes we get lost in the moment, and drift away into our thoughts. This happens to me most mornings when I'm in the shower. I completely zone out. I drift away into my thoughts, and before I know it, I can't remember if I've used conditioner or how long I've been in there!

The shower is an easy place for a quick meditation. This is a superb way to start the day or wind down, and to be present in the moment rather than drifting off thinking about what work has in store or that bill that just landed on the doormat. This is also an excellent meditation to begin the process of connecting with your Higher Guides, which is something we'll begin to talk about soon and what we'll delve into deeply in the next book. (I haven't even finished this one yet but I'm being told that this will turn into a series. Not only that, I somehow know the day and time I will complete this book. Friday, 14th January 2022, at midday.)

Back to the meditation.

Step into the shower. First of all, feel the water hitting your skin, feel it cascade over your head, open your mouth, feel it warming you while you turn around in a couple of circles, and just enjoy. Next I want you to listen, listen to the sound of the water as it splashes all around you. Connect to the present moment. Feel and hear.

Now concentrate on your breathing. Close your eyes. No need for deep breaths, just notice the natural rhythm of your breath, pay attention to it as the lovely warm water washes over you.

Now, with your eyes still closed, I want you to imagine the water as rainbow-colored light, sparkling and glowing and bursting from the shower head, washing you in goodness. It's cleansing you of any nagging, negative energy that you may have collected throughout the day or woken up with. It is light, it is abundant, it's forever, it's limitless, it pours and pours on you, permeating your skin and making you crystal clear, inside and out. Feel it with your Spirit, feel the light connecting with your inner light and draw it inside you. Now expand it out all around you in a glowing rainbow aura. Out from the top of your head, out of your fingertips. I want you to feel this light inside and all around you and expanding outwards, out of the bathroom, out of your home, out into the world and touching all that you see in your mind's eye. Feel that light shine forth from you, feel that healing rainbow energy shooting to all corners of the world, from your fingertips, from the top of your head, from your heart, in all directions.

All who it touches will feel it too. Their lights will be ignited as it travels across the globe, healing and spreading this rainbow sparkling love.

After a few minutes, I want you to start bringing that light back towards you. Feel it receding, see it in your mind's eye moving back across the planet, back along your street, into the building and back into the shower, back in through the top of your head, back through your fingertips, and back to your heart.

Take a moment.

Feel the water on your skin, see it sparkling in your mind's eyes, this shower of light cascading all over you. Listen to the sound it makes. Pay attention to your breathing once more. Now open your eyes.

Do this exercise as often as you like. It is safe, it is nothing but positive, it is your introduction to your Higher Self.

Chapter Six

Time Out

When I was 36 years old, my mum inherited a little bit of money from an old will left to her by her father. One thing she had always wanted to do was go on a Caribbean cruise. And she wanted me to go with her. I remember lining up in Southampton to get on the boat, and looking at a sea of grey-haired heads before us. My mum seemed slightly apprehensive also. We'd taken holidays together before, usually to Miami in the years following my time there, and she certainly wasn't someone who fit in with the golden oldies brigade we were presented with now. We were used to going to rock concerts. In 2010 I'd bought us front row tickets to watch Bon Jovi at the O2 Arena in London. Kid Rock was opening the gig, and my mum had no clue who he was (probably like most people today). I remember the weirdest exchange between them, when he looked down at the front row and made eye contact with my mum, who stood with her arms folded, unimpressed by this dude who wasn't Jon Bon Jovi. He looked genuinely perplexed as to why a 66-year-old English lady was in the front row of his gig. It was hilarious.

We travelled across the Atlantic and to what seemed like countless Caribbean islands and South American towns. Antigua, Barbuda, Barbados, Grenada, Honduras, Mexico, and Panama, among others. We hit Madeira both on the way there and back, and over two months we had the loveliest time in each other's company. Of course, she would drive me nuts sometimes and I'd have to go on my own little excursions. But we went zip-lining in Honduras, waterskiing in Barbados, and she took off one day on a jet ski (at 67 years old and with a heart condition and high blood pressure!) in Aruba. We enjoyed the onboard shows and meals and parties. It really was the trip of a lifetime, and I'm so thankful we shared those memories together. It was also a period of great reflection for me. And given my new calmer outlook on things, I was reevaluating what was important in life and how I had been living until that point. I took some time out and began to slow down. After the cruise, I continued to travel a lot. Miami, South East Asia, the south of France, Italy. One of my best friends lived in Sardinia and I would go for long walks on empty beaches and concentrate on my fitness and mental health. I stayed at hostels in Nice and Rome, and wandered the cities at night soaking up the history and cultures. My next spiritual lesson was on the horizon, one that would lead to the beginnings of my greatest shift of awareness and change the course of my life, but not before it had smashed my ego to smithereens and made me battle for my own sanity.

By 2014 I'd slipped back into bad habits. I was single again, back in Helsinki and drinking heavily. I was supplementing my Personal Training business with working in a bar at the weekends. And on one random and seemingly uneventful morning, I experienced a shocking call to action disguised as a potential psychotic break.

I'd woken up in my apartment with a hangover and random people asleep around me. I'd been out the night before in Helsinki, nothing too eventful; I don't recall anything of the night in question now. It was summer, and through boredom, complacency, and once again a lack of direction, I was hitting the town regularly and pissing each day away into the next. The people I woke up with that morning collected their things, said goodbye and went wherever it was they went. They'd just left when I was musing over something or other, and like a bolt out of the blue it hit me: There's only one constant moment of now. It's the only way we experience things. It's now all the time.

I probably wasn't in the best state of mind to be entertaining such notions, hungover and in limbo with my general direction in life, but nevertheless here it was. And in hindsight, it wouldn't surprise me if I someday learn that what followed wasn't deliberately orchestrated to bring us to the point of me writing this book and you reading it. In fact I am certain of it.

It wasn't like this time concept was a new idea. I'm sure I'd thought of it before. I certainly wasn't the first. But not only did it hit me, it suddenly grabbed hold of me and thrust me in it. I'll try and explain.

The standard, accepted view of our lives, is that we are born, we continue along a life path, and we die. There's a beginning, a middle, and an end, irrespective of how long we may live. Pretty much everything is set up like that. We perceive time moving at a steady pace, it is what it is. It doesn't appear to move any faster than it has to, it doesn't slow down, it moves at a constant speed on a linear course to which we are all aligned and helplessly synchronized. There is no choice. It is happening and we are in it. We flow ever forward towards a nonnegotiable end. We measure it, we divide it into decades, years, months, days, minutes, seconds, and nondescript moments. It makes sense to make sense of it. We compartmentalize and categorize the day to create order. We need to do this to get things done, and we imagine a linear process that once began at the beginning with a big bang and is dotted with notable events in the past as we all jump on for the ride. We see clear evidence of the linear nature of time as we watch ourselves and those we love grow old and infirm. We watch the sun rise and set and the seasons change. We experience everything as a linear flow and we are its passengers. We are able to move at different speeds within it, but there is only the physical passage of time itself to which we have no other option than to succumb to and be part of.

Until we don't.

On that groggy, summer morning, drifting along aimlessly and pretty much just living moment to moment with no end goal in sight, my consciousness suddenly switched gears on me, without warning.

It hit me that we have no choice other than to experience only the present moment. That other moment has just passed, and this one too is about to vanish, as you read these words, along your personal timeline of events. Yet we share this timeline too. We have a collective agreement that this or that happened in the past and this or that event is on the horizon. Somewhere back there along the timeline, we have all of these things that have already happened, forever frozen and mostly agreed upon from our own individual perspectives. But where did those moments physically go? They were just right here. We only have the memory of the moment. We only have this present new moment to experience. And now that's gone too, as we move constantly forward, creating memories instantly and incessantly as each moment passes and then the next and then the next and then the next arrives.

Well, this realization hit me like a ton of bricks. It wasn't limited to an idea either. Something shifted in me physically, I felt hyperaware of my own body and place on the planet. I was me, looking at me. And by me, I mean the one in the background that we've talked about, the one that's usually sitting quietly, unobtrusively, watching and un-judging. Suddenly I was that me, looking at the one who was hungover and having weird thoughts and a panic attack, the background me watching the other me's thoughts but feeling the emotional attachment to them also.

I was jolted out of my old way of thinking. Drifting along with my own ideals of the future and memories of the past, contemplating this or that, moving ever forward without being fully present, suddenly that was stripped away and I was plucked out of the life I had been living for almost 39 years to that point. It was as though a veil had been lifted. I felt stripped bare, my constructs of the world were torn away, I was thrown naked into the harsh, glaring light of ultimate reality. The soft, drifting, mindless scrolling through one day to the next was now gone. There was a new reality to face and it arrived as quickly as a light switch being thrown. Snap. Welcome to the new world. It was terrifying.

People talk about living in the now. Books have been written about the power of it. I'd never read any of them. I still haven't. Being Present. Living In The Moment. The Art Of Now. And the big one: Mindfulness. I'd heard these catchy labels. I knew that people strived to attain this elusive experience, if only for a few seconds of the day. How do I start living and stop worrying? How do I align myself with the present moment? How can I anchor myself in the now? These were suddenly things I didn't have to worry about anymore. Not that I ever had to begin with.

I felt overwhelmed. I felt like I was going mad. I jumped up, threw on some clothes, plugged my headphones into my phone and went for a walk. It was late morning and I headed to the sea, which was nearby my apartment. I remember desperately trying to ignore this prevailing thought, this now now now now now is the only way I can describe it. In hindsight it was actually more like awareness, awareness, awareness. I couldn't switch it off, it was visceral, it was real. In fact nothing had ever felt more visceral or more real ever before. And as wonderful as hindsight is now, at the time I was concerned for my mental health. I wasn't aware that my consciousness had taken the reins. I feared I might be having a psychotic break or the beginnings of schizophrenia. I turned up the music on my phone and tried to concentrate on it, but it didn't help. Each note of the song, the flowing rhythmic pace only reinforced the sense of every moment constantly falling away into the ether, vanished, or frozen in the past, unable to be reclaimed. I walked and walked and looked a few hundred meters ahead and imagined myself over there in a couple of minutes' time, in the future. But where was *that* future coming from? Where was it at *this* moment now? It hadn't happened yet. All that was happening was now, I thought. There was ultimately no future, only a theory of it, or an expectation. We know it's coming, there is nowhere but forward, but we only really experience the present moment. All the time.

I began to panic. I marched onwards thinking that soon this way of thinking would pass. But it didn't. I was experiencing an ultimate awareness. I couldn't switch it off. There was only the present moment of now and I was trapped in it. I couldn't drift off into my thoughts and wonder what I was going to eat for dinner that evening or reflect on the day before. It was now. Always and forever. And it didn't stop.

After much reflection on this experience (which was constant for the better part of a year from that morning), research into meditative states, and others' accounts of an "awakening", I've come to the conclusion that what I was experiencing was a glimpse into a higher reality. A reality that exists on a usually subtler plane than our standard senses can perceive. I had moved beyond my nervous system's usual mode of functioning, and into a greater awareness of self and connection to mostly unperceived vibrational frequencies. The indigenous Shamans of Northern America called it the "eternal now". A gigantic tapestry of everything that ever has been or will be stretching in every direction. Primordial time. A deathless awareness of the everlasting now. The speed with which I had moved to this new awareness was too much for my logical mind and ego to comprehend, and it sent me into an almost continuous state of panic.

Chapter Seven

Back To The Future

I could barely function. I went to work at the bar, but if it got too busy I became overwhelmed and had to step out for a few minutes. I felt ultra-sensitive to absolutely everything. I felt fragile, like my mind was made of crystal and was zinging along to a new frequency. My ego couldn't take it. It wasn't in control anymore. It had been pounded to the ground and kept there. I went to work out at the gym, thinking that throwing myself into physical pursuits would give my brain a break and distract it with the mundane effort of lifting and banging weights around. No such luck. I saw a friend on the street one day and I could barely speak with him. I'd been sitting contemplating this new perspective on things and trying not to let it freak me out. He was with his new girlfriend and they walked away confused and concerned. I tried to explain to people what I was going through, and each time was met with the same look of sympathy and befuddlement. It just didn't stop. I was constantly living in the present moment and it was horrific. I saw no choice but to go and speak with a doctor. Maybe prescription drugs would help. I'd already tried drinking it away but it just made things worse. The hangovers only amplified the self-awareness.

The doctor used the word "psychosis". She repeatedly asked me if I had been using mind-altering drugs. She didn't seem to believe me when I said I hadn't. She prescribed me antianxiety medication that I should take if my episodes became too overwhelming. Except they weren't episodes, they were a constant, ever-present onslaught of the present. There was no escaping it. I developed a new way of looking at the world, at this construct of time that we have set up. What if there was no such thing as linear time? What if it was more like a time spiral?

Forever in motion, moving neither up nor down nor sideways, but just always now and forever? That would mean that everything that had ever happened was happening right now, and maybe everything that ever could happen was happening also. Which meant multiple universes. Which didn't really help me feel much better. But it made a little more sense to me to look at reality this way. But then it didn't fit in with the fact that things definitely do move forward. The evidence is all around us. We plant a seed in a pot of soil and water it, we watch the plant grow, we watch it eventually die. Things move from A to B. But no matter, I could no longer experience that concept because it wasn't the experience I was having. I realized that none of us are actually living in the past or the future because there is nothing but The Forever Now.

This paradox of time being both linear and spiral somehow helped me make sense of it. Trying to explain it to people was met with blank stares and awkwardness. I went to another doctor. Once again, the prognosis was psychosis, albeit "mild" since I was still functioning day to day and holding down two jobs. The word psychosis scared the crap out of me. I continued to experience a constant, low pulse of pure panic. A panic attack that lasted 24/7. I'd wake up and be in it, and it would throb and thrive all day until I medicated myself to sleep.

I went home to England. I went to stay with my mum. She had been living alone now for a long time with her cute little dog called Sukie, a Japanese Chin. She had just turned seventy years old and would go for long walks with Sukie on the beach which kept her active and healthy, and helped with her blood pressure and heart condition. Walks on the beach with my mum and Sukie seemed exactly what I needed. To go back to the house where I grew up, to be in familiar and comfortable surroundings.

I remember my mum took a picture of me while we walked on the beach. It was late summer and I wore a grey hoodie and jeans, and I leaned against a wooden groin that divided the sand with my hood pulled up, arms folded and head down. That picture sums up exactly where my head was at, at the time. I was trapped inside, listening to the constant reminder that nothing actually made sense anymore.

My mum was naturally concerned for me. But when I tried to explain what I was going through, she gave me that same look that everyone else who I attempted to explain things to gave me, albeit with more concern and compassion. Nevertheless I attempted to live a normal life. During that same trip, I went with a friend of mine who lived in London to watch an interactive and immersive experience of the movie *Back to the Future*. I'm aware of the irony. It was a wonderful experience and allowed me to somewhat get away from the intrusive awareness of the moment of now. It was a welcome distraction. The entire movie set of *Back to the Future* had been recreated, complete with working diner, bars, shops, and actors playing the residents of Hill Valley, the town from the film. Throughout the day the actors would perform various scenes, moving the story along chronologically before they eventually screened the movie itself on the front of a recreated full-sized clocktower. It was the first time in a couple of months that I was actually able to be distracted for a little while, and it was bliss.

I wanted that again. I just wanted to return to the herd and worry about my next paycheck or a new wrinkle on my face or what was happening in the next episode of my favorite TV show. I'd had enough of this insight into a different realm existing within this one. Because that's what it was. The universe had decided it was time for me to wake up. I'd wasted enough time sliding in and out of relationships with different women and frittering my life away on partying. I was being reminded that I perhaps have a natural insight into things that a lot of people don't. It was a harsh, metaphysical slap in the face. It was time to stop wasting time, and how better to remind me of that than by demonstrating what time wasn't. The only problem was, everyone else thought I had cracked. No one else seemed to have a damned clue what I was talking about. Well, almost no one else.

When I returned to Helsinki, I went to talk with the one man who I hoped might be able to get my brain back on to this plane. A few years earlier, I'd spoken with a therapist named Juha Rainio who had helped me immensely with jealous behavior stemming from my unresolved issues with my stepfather. He'd helped me clearly see why I was behaving the way I was, why I was growing increasingly possessive in my relationship, and why I was drinking heavily and being unreliable. But back to my consciousness conundrum. You see I wasn't looking at what was happening to me at that moment with the hindsight I have now. I kind of understood that I was experiencing something bigger than me and my perceived point of view of my place in the world. But mostly I thought I was going nuts. Along with a lot of people who knew me. I was getting to the point that if my brain was going to continue working the way that it was, then I didn't want to be around anymore. I genuinely couldn't take it. It was a living nightmare. It was as though I had stepped outside of myself, and was watching and listening to every single thought that passed through my brain intently while being completely and utterly detached from them, yet there I was, having them! It was madness. It wasn't mindfulness, it was a complete dissolution from the self, while simultaneously still experiencing the self. There wasn't a moment's rest. And I was beginning to doubt my sanity.

Juha sat listening to me in silence while I begged and pleaded with him to make it all go away. His eyes narrowed behind his glasses, and when I told him I thought I was schizophrenic he gave me a slight smile.

"You're too old to develop schizophrenia," he told me

casually in his monotone Finnish accent. "But to treat this issue traditionally," he went on. "We would need an anchor point to start with, an event that triggered the trauma, and from what you have said, there isn't one."

I was deflated. He was my only hope. I seriously couldn't conceive of functioning normally on a day-to-day basis when my mind felt like it were spiraling out of control.

"But what you're saying makes perfect sense to me," Juha continued. "I do understand what you're going through. You've had a shift in awareness, you're experiencing something that most people don't experience. It's what's known as a breakthrough, but not in the traditional sense of the word. Right now, you fear that you are losing your grip on reality, when the truth is, you are actually seeing reality. Perhaps for the first time. You see, I believe that you are a mystic, and you have just started your journey."

I watched him for a long moment without saying anything.

What had he just said? Did he just call me a "mystic"? What was that supposed to mean?

"But you want to get back to the herd," he went on. "You want that to make sense again," he pointed to the clock on the wall. I nodded.

"You want to join the rest of them out there going about their daily business," he said. "And with that, I can help you."

I breathed a sigh of relief.

He told me to close my eyes. Thank God. Maybe he was going to hypnotize me or something, I thought. All of this will go away and I can go back to living my life like I was before. I want to take the blue pill. I want to be part of the crowd. I want to live in contented ignorance. I don't like any of this.

But he didn't hypnotize me. Instead, he talked me through a guided meditation, a meditation that helped me immensely. I was so willing to go along with anything that could help, I almost fell into a trance during it. He talked me through a beautiful grounding exercise that I adapted earlier in this book (The Mountain and The Mirror). It is a very calming and sturdy exercise, and after the very first time doing it, I felt a huge wave of relief wash over me.

On the tram going home, I genuinely felt that the grounding meditation had brought me back to a mundane existence once again, although I knew it would only be temporary. Juha had warned me of that. The effects wouldn't last, since I was going through such a powerful awakening. I cannot impress with words what it was I was going through. You'll find that, as you go on. Ultimate awareness of consciousness, or so-called mystical experiences, are very difficult to relay in words. Sometimes next to impossible. David Joseph Bohm, one of the most significant theoretical physicists of the 20th century, who attempted to understand the nature of reality and consciousness, had a wonderful quote about it.

Our greatest obstacle to understanding consciousness is our language.

Our demonstrative and fragmented means of thought and expression do not serve us beyond the everyday mundane. I was temporarily back to where I thought I wanted to be. I would have to incorporate the meditation into daily life. I would add other grounding techniques also, and I would see Juha again. But I was on the path to once again living a life of banality.

Obviously it didn't last very long.

Chapter Eight

Flow

A mystic. Juha had called me a mystic. He hadn't said I was going crazy, he hadn't questioned me about taking drugs. He hadn't used the words "temporary psychosis" like the regular doctors had. He'd appeared to know exactly what I was going through, and I'd somehow found the one medical professional in Helsinki that knew how to fix me. We had other conversations, in my subsequent visits. There was a side to this mental health practitioner that he hadn't revealed on my initial visits with him back when I was trying to fix a lack of direction. Now he casually talked about seeing spirits, which at the time I found difficult to believe. He talked about alternate realities and philosophical ideas around my time conundrum. I don't think there could have been a medical professional better suited to help me than that man, and I will forever be grateful to him for helping me through that period. He was a Shaman, plain and simple, and he guided me through the forest and back to the village. And as terrifying as the entire experience was, I am so very thankful now that I went through it.

It was during this time that I pondered what might have been, had I given more attention and fairness to a brief relationship I'd had a year or so before. I'd met and fallen for a lovely girl named Laura, and we'd dated for a couple of months. But my on-again, off-again ex had returned from an extended period living in Rome, and I unceremoniously dumped Laura in favor of trying to rekindle a relationship that I had mostly been responsible for dismantling. Having been single through my year of apparent enlightenment, I would often think of what might have been if the relationship with Laura had blossomed. To cut a long story short, I begged her forgiveness, she let me sweat awhile, and we moved to London.

My mum had recently undergone a minor operation that went majorly wrong, and she took weeks to recover. Added to that, the people who were looking after her dog while she recovered vanished, with the dog. She grew lonely. She didn't have her routine morning walks to the beach with Sukie anymore. She slowly recovered. But not completely.

Laura and I settled in West London, in a place called Richmond. We absolutely adored living in Richmond, and still do. With the winding Thames and cobblestone streets, its riverside pubs and acres of park. Twenty minutes from Central London yet a million miles away when you need to escape the bustle of the city. And I was only a two-hour train journey and short boat trip down to the Isle of Wight. I felt good being back in England. I was home again, and Laura was enjoying living in a foreign country. I saw an ad for a part-time drama school and auditioned for it, and the next thing I knew I was rehearsing Chekhov in a school in Camden every week. Halfway through my first year studying acting, I landed a small role on a Netflix show. Forty years on, and I was finally doing what I'd first wanted to do, and working in the film industry. All with seemingly little effort on my part. An acceptance of what was for me, wouldn't go by me. Not sweating the small stuff. Being aware of my thoughts, and observing. All stemming from what could be described as either a spiritual awakening, or a psychotic break. The deep understanding that time is a constant spiral rather than something which is running out, freed me up to realize it's never too late. It resonated with me so intimately, worked its way into my core and clung to me so intently, that I could turn it off and on at will. If I found myself drifting aimlessly in my thoughts and that life was passing me by, I could snap myself into the moment and be ultra-present without the existential crisis that had previously accompanied it.

Mystic?

I'd almost forgotten about that word.

I'd been so caught up living in the moment, enjoying our new life, keeping a close eye on my mother, getting small roles on TV shows and beginning to tentatively call myself an actor, that I'd forgotten all about Astral Planes and Spirit Guides. I was purposefully living in the now, it became a way of life rather than a conscious effort. I'd opened multiple new doors, and life was creeping up on me again and keeping me distracted. But it's also funny how your soul's purpose knows what's best no matter what. Sooner or later it will remind you again. And again. And one day, you have to listen.

Meditation Exercise: Breathe and Glow.
Level: Beginner

Find a quiet space, where you won't be disturbed for five minutes. Sit comfortably with your back straight and your feet on the floor. Relax. Close your eyes, and take a couple of deep breaths. Now begin to concentrate solely on your breath, as it returns to its normal rhythm.

I want you to start to imagine that you are surrounded by a soft, glowing light, and with each breath, pull that light into your lungs.

As you breathe and pull in the light, I want you to see it travel from your lungs out to the rest of your body. See it expanding from the center of your chest, out and up into your throat, across your shoulders, down your arms, and into your fingertips. Feel your body grow warm as the light travels down your arms. Feel the warmth soften your stomach as it moves down through it. Feel it lighting up your groin and travelling into each leg, down around your knees, warming any tension that might be collected there. Feel it travel down through your calves, around your ankles, and into your feet and toes.

With each breath push the light a little further. See it travel up into your head and into the darkest corners of your mind. Where there may be negative energy and thoughts, let the light blast those corners wide open and expose them, brightening everything until there is nothing but the light itself. Let your mind grow weightless as it glows bright, and feel it rise upwards just above your head.

Sit in this power. Feel the glow. Begin to expand the light further from your body and into the room or area where you sit. You are a glowing ball of light, emanating nothing but warmth and positivity.

When you feel that your mind begins to wander, concentrate on your breath and pulling that light inside, then expand it outwards.

After a few minutes, I want you to pull the light back towards you. See it travelling back up from your toes, back around your calves and up towards your torso. Feel it having cleansed the mind, travelling back down your neck and towards your center. Feel it moving back up your arms towards your chest.

When you have collected the light at your center, begin to pay attention to your breath once more. Become aware of the sounds around you, out on the street or in the park. Tap your feet on the floor and wiggle your fingers.

Keep the light collected in your chest for the remains of the day. It will dissipate naturally as you go about your business.

Open your eyes.

Welcome back.

Chapter Nine

Rainbow Guides

It was probably around midday when I began to stir out of sleep. Someone was telling me something in a dream. Actually, multiple people were, way smarter than me. And come to think of it, they weren't people at all, and I wasn't dreaming.

I was awake and fully conscious, and a collective voice was asking me a profound question.

"Do you still want this? Are you ready to receive this?"

I panicked. I was outside of myself and could see a rainbow stream shooting directly into the top of my head as I looked at myself, laying there. I felt that old spinning feeling again, the one from twenty years before when we'd been dabbling with Ouija boards. Timelessness, just like before, nothing existing before or after and that revelation once again that we live in nothing but the everlasting moment of Now. I was being uploaded with information, a direct stream into the top of my head, information about things beyond my understanding, things that would change everything for me, and I panicked.

"No, no, no!" I screamed in my mind. And no sooner had I said it, the rainbow stream stopped and the connection was broken.

I opened my eyes.

Between myself and the ceiling was a holographic, glowing orange grid. More rust colored actually, than orange. Just hovering there, in the space between me and the ceiling of our bedroom.

Interesting.

I simply lay there and watched it. It was there for maybe twenty seconds. I blinked. It was still there. I rubbed my eyes and opened them again. Still there. And then slowly it began to fade until it completely vanished.

I sat up and climbed out of bed.

That was intense. I felt elated. I hadn't anticipated such a thing happening. What could it have been? Nothing like this had happened in years. I did what anyone in a committed relationship would do and I called my fiancée, since she was in Helsinki visiting family.

"It sounds like you were dreaming," she said, after I relayed what happened.

"Look, I know it sounds crazy," I told her. "But I swear, I was wide awake. This rainbow stream of information was shooting into the top of my head. And beings smarter than myself were trying to tell me something." It sounded perfectly reasonable to me at the time. It had just happened. But Laura was having none of it.

"Maybe just try and go back to sleep," she suggested. "You had a late night working and you've got a busy day ahead."

Alright. This wouldn't do. I called one of my best friends, Matt. We'd been seeing a lot of each other since he lived close-by to my London address.

"Were you drinking last night?" he asked me after I told him about the direct stream of rainbow consciousness that had attached itself to my head.

"I swear, man, I wasn't drunk and I wasn't dreaming," I told him. "Or well, I was dreaming, but then I came out of it. And the grid, I was fully and wide awake when I saw the grid. It was glowing like a hologram, and then it disappeared."

"Maybe you slept funny," Matt suggested. "Like if your eye was squeezed into your arm and you were just seeing traces when you woke up."

"I was on my back," I insisted. But it was no use. Neither he nor Laura believed me. And fair enough, I admit it sounded pretty nuts. Even reading what I've written here looks bonkers, and if I hadn't experienced it, I might think it was bonkers too.

The next day, I took a walk through Richmond Park and eventually settled on a bench on Richmond Hill, and I did what I was surprised I hadn't already done. I took out my phone and Googled it.

...seeing a grid upon waking...
...rainbow stream into head...

You wouldn't think much would come up on either of those things, would you? Well. It turned out I wasn't the only one.

So the first suggestions were glaucoma, or myodesopsia, both down to ageing eyes and attributed to seeing patterns and floaters upon waking or at other times throughout the day. But this didn't really match my experience. And the fact that I'd seen the grid immediately after seemingly receiving information from Higher Evolved Beings than myself was too much of a coincidence. I went on. And then I started getting to the good stuff.

Waking up to glimpses of a digital world. Sacred geometry. Geometric organizers of the universe. These were some of the rabbit holes I stumbled down when researching my experience. But nothing about the rainbow stream of consciousness shooting information directly in to the top of my head. With medical explanations off the table (none of them mirrored my experience), I began to find some interesting threads about people who claimed they saw holographic grids when looking out to sea. Or one intriguing story of a teenage boy waking to hear static noise coming from his brother's bedroom at night. The next morning he brought it up at breakfast. "Did you leave your TV on? I woke up at 3am and could hear loud static coming from your room." The other brother answered no, but he had also woken at exactly 3am to see a glowing holographic grid all around him.

The only thing I could find online about cosmic Supra-

Conscious rainbows was a digital picture for a music genre called Vaporwave. There was a humanoid shape floating in space with a rainbow going into the top of its head and a glowing grid over the whole image. I mean that was pretty close, to be honest. I read on and came across a New Age forum where all of the participants were in agreement that glimpses of grids were simply seeing through the veil of reality and to the real mechanics of nonphysical creation. This was all truly fascinating. But nothing had really changed in my life since this experience. As the weeks went on I often pondered what would have happened if I hadn't panicked and answered yes, I am ready, for whatever information was being downloaded to my subconscious when asked. And I was certain that whoever had done the asking were of a profoundly greater intelligence than myself. Of that I am without a doubt.

No one asked again. But that's not to say they stopped talking entirely.

Chapter Ten

Perception Shapes Potential

As we change our perception, we can alter what we believe to be possible. When what we believe to be possible changes or expands, the energy of our mind changes and expands, and connects to that of Higher Consciousness. Many people find it difficult to put such trust in what appears to be a flaky notion. And I get it, I truly get it. Even after everything that I've described so far, all of the signs and moments of clarity and even the better part of a year readjusting to a new way of perceiving reality, I've *still* slipped back into habitual ways of thinking. I've still gotten caught up in worrying about the mundane, paying bills, stressing about barely making the rent, getting frustrated with London traffic, being disappointed by my favorite TV show's latest episode. All thoughts of tuning in to my highest version of myself or Spirit Guides on Astral Planes get lost within the practicalities of day-to-day living. I may sound as though I'm walking around like Yoda, but I can assure you that much of my day is still spent wondering when my last remittance will be cleared. Life is hard. It's *hard*. We get caught up in dramas, don't get enough sleep, eat badly, have deadlines to meet, get ill, people let us down, we let others down, we beat ourselves up over our shortcomings, we have to pay the bills, and it goes on and on and somewhere among all that, we have to make time to meditate and talk to invisible beings who may or may not even exist? Go easy on yourself. You have to. Taking time out to meditate isn't a chore, but I promise you, our monkey brains will convince us that it is. I had a spare hour today that I planned to devote purely to meditating, and guess what my brain did? It found 25 other things that suddenly needed to be done at the exact same time. I started loading the dishwasher, I picked up a pair of dumbbells lying around and squeezed in a few lateral shoulder raises. Then I thought if I'm doing shoulder raises I may as well chug a protein shake so I mixed one up. I quickly checked Instagram and found a voice message from an old friend who was feeling low and needed someone to talk to, and before I knew it, that hour set aside for meditating was soon gone and I had to meet Laura from work as we had dinner plans. My ego didn't want me to meditate. It likes things the way they are. The brain chatter started. The what about this and the what about that. We are primarily living in a physical world and we set things up a long, long time ago to keep it that way. We needed to survive. We need to eat. Stuff needs to be done. But I implore you. Step back. Take the time. You won't grow spiritually without being able to switch the chatter off and shut the ego down. Even if you only do it for five minutes a day. Or five minutes every two days. To walk this path, you need to give yourself the time to do it. To connect with your Higher Self, you need to give yourself the space to do it. To hear your Spirit Guides, you need to create the silence for them to be heard. To manifest a destiny, you need to turn down the incessant imposing thoughts that will block, entangle, and confuse the process. And when you finally begin to accomplish these things, and get results, you'll be so amazed at how smoothly life begins to flow that you'll want to shout it from the rooftops, you'll want your loved ones and friends to know all about it and begin living this way themselves! You'll want to share the joy! And you'll tell them about this wonderful new way of living, and they'll look at you like you're nuts.

Here's the thing. Your Spirit Guides will continue keeping an eye on you, whether you believe in them or not. You'll manifest your own destiny, whether you do it consciously or not. The All That Is will continue to be The All That Is, whether you choose to align with it or not. You will live your life and one day reach the end of it, regardless of if you live a life of awareness or one of complacency. You will get to where you are going, there is zero doubt about it. But shall you flow towards it, or stumble blindly forwards, sideways, and occasionally backwards?

There is a Slip-Stream Super Highway running alongside you right now, you only have to decide if you'll jump on for the ride.

Perception shapes potential. Try it. Quiet the mind, let the marching band of thoughts march right on by. They won't stop, they'll keep going, they'll keep vying for your attention as they pass, but after you begin to quietly acknowledge them and let them wander on without attaching any emotion or actions to them, they'll tone it right down for awhile and give you a moment's peace. You. The one who is observing them. You, the one who is always quietly watching from the background. You, the one who knows the answer immediately before the ego creates all of the buts, whys, and maybes. The voice that cuts through all of the crap in moments of crisis. The knowing that has known all along and reaches out to the Higher Awareness that is always ready to align with you and make your thoughts a reality. Give yourself time to meditate, and you will begin to know you again. Create a new perspective on life, and shape new possibilities. Just try it. But find those quiet moments.

Chapter Eleven

Evidence

Smarter people than myself have reached the same conclusions that we are headed towards in this book. Walk in to any bookstore and to the shelves labelled "Mind, Body, and Spirit", and you'll find an abundance of books on meditation, mindfulness, tarot cards, ghosts, Chakras, auras, and pretty much anything else covered in esoteric writings. But despite many people beginning to embrace the idea of Spirituality as something more than woo-woo pseudoscience mumbo jumbo, there are still many who believe the latter. What fascinates and delights me, is when people educated as scientists, doctors, and physicians who previously dismissed any notions of esoteric studies as fantasy have their own experiences that defy their analytical understanding.

Marjorie Hines Woollacott is a retired American neuroscientist and professor who had an extremely practical outlook on life, and no doubt that our human experience was purely governed by a brain reliant on chemicals and electrical impulses. That was until she began meditating, and was forced to question her own analytical research about what causes human consciousness. After rejecting her peers, she made the case for an expanded scientific paradigm in which consciousness is primary. In her book, *Infinite Awareness*, Marjorie documents her own experience of what she calls infinite awareness through meditation, with research in to consciousness that can't be explained within the prevailing and scientifically accepted materialist paradigm. She also points out how seemingly intangible experiences through meditation can physically transform the brain, suggesting that consciousness precedes matter.

American psychiatrist Dr. Raymond Moody coined the

phrase Near Death Experience (NDE) in his groundbreaking book *Life After Life*, which was published in 1975. With a BA, MA, PhD and later MD to his name, he worked as a professor and forensic scientist. After interviewing over a thousand people on the subject of patients returning to life after being pronounced physically dead, he became convinced that our consciousness continues after our bodies die. He travelled the world and spoke with people of different backgrounds and religions who had died and returned to life, and decided that the cases were overwhelmingly similar in description despite individual beliefs and cultural upbringing. It would be fair to point out that Moody's career hasn't been without controversy, and he has received a fair share of criticism due to his research being based on anecdotal evidence. Nevertheless, he remains a pioneer in the field of NDE research, and a learned mind that has dropped the need of approval from his peers in favor of following his own undeniable truth.

Wernher von Braun was a German-American aerospace engineer and space architect. After working with the Nazis in WWII, he secretly escaped Germany as part of "Operation Paperclip", and became a pioneer of rocket and space technology in the US. "Science has found that nothing can disappear without a trace," he said, on the subject of life after death. "Nature does not know extinction. All it knows is transformation. Doesn't it make sense to assume that applies to the human soul? I think it does. And everything science has taught me – and continues to teach me – strengthens my belief in the continuity of our spiritual existence after death. Nothing disappears without a trace."

In 2008, Dr. Eben Alexander, an academic neurosurgeon and self-proclaimed atheist, was put into a medically-induced coma due to bacterial meningitis. His doctors put his survival rate at below 10%. Not only did he make a full and miraculous recovery, he also maintained and recounted a profound Near

Death Experience, after the neocortex of his brain had been completely shut down. He has since gone on to write three best-selling books on the subject of NDEs and consciousness.

The list could go on and on. Equally impressive, are those who have no background in the sciences, or religious upbringings at all. Everyday people, who were going about their ordinary lives, have received a call to spiritual action from out of the blue and gone on to become some of our greatest teachers on the subjects of spirituality and consciousness.

Neale Donald Walsch began writing his *Conversations with God* books following one crushing event after another, resulting in him being divorced, with a broken neck, and homeless.

Gordon Smith was a barber in Scotland who was told that one day he would be a medium, by a family friend. He has since gone on to write over fifteen books, frequently sells out worldwide tours in which he demonstrates his mediumistic abilities, and has been labelled Britain's most accurate medium.

Yamile Yemoonyah is a professional Spirit Guide medium, spiritual teacher, best-selling author and founder of the Spirit Guide Society. She has helped thousands of people connect with their own Spirit Guides through private readings, courses, and workshops. Her first spiritual experience didn't occur until she was at university, when one of her guides appeared to her late at night in her room. Her second experience was when she woke up from an afternoon nap while living in Barcelona, and believed that she was being downloaded with information from a source beyond herself. So far, she is the only person I know of that I share this experience with. The information she received went on to form the basis for her best-selling book, *The Seven Types of Spirit Guide*.

Chapter Twelve

A Change Of Pace

The further I progress on this journey, the more information I receive and experiences that I have, the more I am convinced that each and every one of us have the ability to explore and unquestionably know our higher consciousness. It's simply a matter of tuning in. Now, not everyone has the calls to action that I have written about here, and continue to have. It took me until I was 45 years old to wake up and answer them. But that doesn't mean you don't already have that inner knowing that there is more to life than what we have been shown so far. A knowing. A guidance. A spark. An experience that doesn't fit in with every other experience you've had. Perhaps if you've had an experience like that, it doesn't sit in your memory the same way that everything else does. Perhaps something out of the ordinary happened, something that you dismissed because it didn't add up, so you chose to ignore it and return to the everyday mundane. And when you recall it now it still doesn't quite make sense. But there's an undeniable knowing within that confirms it happened.

It took such an experience to accelerate my own spiritual growth. Even after everything I've already recounted here, I easily fell back into the everyday humdrum of reality. I was living in London and finally realizing my dreams of working in the film industry. I finished drama school and began another. I was loving it. Acting took me out of my comfort zones, and opened up an entire world of possibilities and opportunities. In 2019, I went for a small audition as a featured background artist for an upcoming period television show called *The Great*, starring Elle Fanning in the title role of Catherine the Great. We filmed Season One over a scattered eight months, and I was getting regular work. I was earning less money than I'd grown used to as a Personal Trainer back in Helsinki, but in all honesty I was happier, and that made the world of difference. Even working as an extra, I felt I was finally on track for what I'd always secretly wanted to do. I landed an acting job with an actual character name and dialogue for a Netflix show about pirates, and managed to squeeze that in between days on *The Great*. And have no doubt about it, it was no coincidence that this happened directly after my shift in awareness helped me flow forward with less resistance. I'd stopped sweating the small stuff. Money was tight, but I trusted myself enough to know that I wouldn't ever completely screw things up to the point of getting into financial trouble. Also, Laura was about to complete three years of university as a mature student, and had steady employment with a reasonable wage. Between the two of us, we were going to be fine.

I completed filming *The Great* with a week in Caserta, Italy, where we shot all of the external scenes of the palace featured in the show. It was March 2020, and for a few months there'd been talk of a virus called COVID-19 that had originated in China. I'd largely ignored it after living through the previous eras of Swine Flu and Aviation Flu unscathed, plus I selfishly assumed it was South East Asia's problem, not Europe's. But going through the airport in Caserta, things appeared to be ramping up. Now, I was an over seasoned plane boarding expert by this point. I'd had a period of flying back and forth to Helsinki every week during our first year in London, training a couple of my PT clients. But this day was different. For a start, the staff at the little airport in Caserta were wearing biohazard suits. That seemed a little extreme to me at the time. We'd just spent a week filming with large crowds in close proximity to one another, spent our evenings sharing pizzas and wine with the cast and crew, yet here were the passport control people looking like the guys who take E.T. away from Elliott at the end of the movie.

They took our temperatures with a digital thermometer, and ushered us on to the plane.

Back in the UK I immediately had a couple of days' work on a big superhero movie through Sony and Marvel. And then a further few days on a TV show called *Britannia* which was filming at an old Roman farm close to Portsmouth. I stayed in a roadside hotel near to the site of the farm, and after the first day of filming I collapsed into a warm and comfortable bed. At some point in the night I woke to the sound of the floorboards creaking in my room. Because the hotel was out in the middle of nowhere, there was no external light coming through the curtained windows. I couldn't see a thing, and then I heard the noise again, right at the bottom of my bed.

I sat up, and peered into the pitch black. It was so beyond dark, that even after sleeping for a few hours my eyes couldn't adjust or see a thing. The noise again, at the bottom of my bed, and with it the creepy feeling that someone was standing there. Not only that, a weird sense that it was someone ancient, male, maybe military? How could I know that? I fumbled for the light at the bedside table, and of course, there was no one standing at the foot of my bed.

I mentioned it back on set the next morning to a couple of different people, and both times I was met with a humored response. I decided to keep it to myself for the rest of the day. The next night in the hotel the floorboards didn't creak and I slept like a baby.

Since I was close to the South Coast of England, I took the opportunity to go and visit with my mum on the Isle of Wight. Looking back now I relish the memory of those times with her. When I was actually living them, I took them for granted. We would go shopping for her weekly groceries together at Marks & Spencer, and we'd have a coffee somewhere and lunch. On rare occasions, we'd go to the cinema and watch something. At 75 years old, her favorite movies to go and watch would be *The Fast and the Furious* franchise. We watched all of the newly released *Star Wars* movies and the Marvel superhero films. She was such fun and easily entertained. But she would also have her dark days, brought on by unresolved experiences from her past, and it was no wonder. She came from an era where people didn't talk about their personal grievances, or the wrongdoings that others had inflicted upon them. She was clinically depressed, and among the multitude of pills she would take for angina, high blood pressure, diverticular disease, thrombosis, and arthritis, she had been on and off antidepressants her entire life.

It was during this trip to the island in March 2020, that I went for a wander around one of my favorite places on the island, Castle Carisbrooke.

The Normans built a motte-and-bailey castle at Carisbrooke around the year 1100. This replaced a temporary castle built soon after the Norman Conquest of 1066. That itself was built on the site of a Saxon fortress that was thought to have been a defense against Viking raids. After being besieged by the French in 1377, the castle eventually became the prison for King Charles I during the English Civil War. Now you can wander freely around its outer walls, or pay to gain entrance to the castle and walk around its battlements and into its rooms and the church within its enclosure.

On my day in March, I opted to wander around the outside of the castle and through the woodland surrounding it. I suddenly became aware of a presence beside me, walking with me. A male energy, a soldier in fact. A young man, from hundreds of years ago. I don't know how I knew this, I just did. I didn't receive anything else, I just felt him. I continued to walk through the woods and I sensed he continued to walk with me. I didn't feel scared, I didn't feel threatened. I didn't feel any sense of urgency or that he wanted to tell me anything. I just simply felt him there until after awhile, he wasn't anymore. Now, despite a similar thing happening only days before at the roadside hotel, and all of the other occurrences that happened which I have already described so far, I immediately doubted what I'd felt. I went back to my mum's house, I forgot about the subtle energy I'd sensed when wandering around the castle, and later when I thought back on it, I put it down to possibly being my imagination. The same with the hotel room. It's so easy to dismiss these moments, especially as it would seem that they don't reside in our memories the same way that ordinary experiences do. Also, these early experiences weren't as palpable as others I've had since. That being said, it was perhaps these two that finally got me thinking that I was possibly predisposed to having things such as these happen. Maybe I should try and actively remember and record what happened, should anything actually happen again.

I talked with my good friend Andy who lives in Italy. We speak most days, or at least we text, since becoming friends in Helsinki nearly twenty years ago. He grew up in a religious environment, and during one of our conversations that March, he happened to tell me about someone from his upbringing who was considered something of a "seer". Some of the things he told me sounded similar to my own experiences, and not long after we spoke, I stumbled upon a book about Shamanism. At exactly the same time, the world began to suffer from the rapid spread of COVID-19. The UK went into its first lockdown, as did much of Europe, and we watched horrified as the television news reports recorded the number of daily deaths at an ever-increasing rate. From the 26th of March, we were told to stay at home, away from our friends and family, and all semblance of regular life came to a halt as cinemas, shops, and restaurants closed their doors. The fear, the unknowing, the uncertainty of what would happen next gripped the world. I wasn't allowed to visit my mum anymore, and as a result she grew increasingly lonely without anyone going to see her at home. I organized for food to be delivered to her from the local supermarkets, since she was in the most vulnerable of age groups in her mid-seventies, and even when restrictions were lifted briefly during June, I thought it safer to keep away lest I unknowingly pass on the virus to her. She began to show symptoms of depression. She was out of her usual routines and habits and sat at home day after day without any social contact other than our daily video calls. In hindsight, I wished I'd have broken the rules and gone to stay with her every damn day.

Chapter Thirteen

Ashram

According to the Oxford English Dictionary, a Shaman is categorized as a person who has access to, and influence in, the Spirit World. The word may date back as far as two millennia, and was used by Western anthropologists to broadly describe magico-religious practices from Asia, Australasia, Africa and parts of the Americas, as they naively believed these practices to be one and the same. The actual origins of Shamanism stem from Northern Europe and parts of Northern Asia. There has been criticism of modern Western interpretations and practices of Shamanic rituals, in the name of cultural misrepresentation and appropriation. Traditionally, Shamans are known as people who practice important culturally recognized ceremonial and social duties. They are those who seek the assistance of the Spirit World to bring knowledge, healing, cosmic order and balance to their people. They believe that each of us are genetically hardwired with a program that allows us to expand our consciousness, and that we simply need to activate it to access our Guides. The term Neoshamanism is used to describe those in the West who have adapted Shamanic rituals to advance personal exploration and spiritual development. Native American communities have criticized modern Neoshamanic practices, with regards to Shamanism playing an important role in native cultures, and calling Western Neoshamans imposters who are involved in cultural appropriation.

I am in no way endorsing being, or suggesting that I am a regular practitioner of either Shamanic or Neoshamanic rituals. But I will share my experience of trying a guided meditation that I found after reading a book on Shamanism, in the summer of 2020. Something that I also learned, and is worth noting, was that the ancient Shamans from Northern Amerindian tribes would talk of seeing a holographic grid when connecting with their Spirit Guides.

Lockdown number one, was a mixed bag of anxiety, uncertainty, and an odd novelty. Good weather in the UK gave us room for nightly back garden barbecues through the Spring and Summer of that year. The daily news briefings were horrific, and I remember the shock of seeing hospital wards at breaking point and the thousands of people attached to breathing machines. It was something that my generation had nothing to compare with. Whereas our grandparents, and to some extent parents, had lived through World Wars, the global pandemic and change of lifestyle was a terrifying venture into the unknown for people my age and younger. But the ones who suffered most, were the elderly who were reaching the end of their lives. It was absolutely and completely unfair that they should have to endure being locked in their own homes and live in fear of a new, invisible and deadly killer at that stage in their lives. But we tried to do the right thing. We stayed at home, we wore masks in public, we went for our allocated daily exercise, and we kept away from the elderly to try and keep them safe.

I was fortunate to have Richmond Park on my doorstep. I could walk out of my front door and be in the woods within minutes. Over seven miles in each direction, and spanning 2,500 acres, it's a wildlife conservation and nature reserve home to over 600 wild deer and countless fluorescent green parakeets. Living in close proximity to Richmond Park is essentially having the benefits of the countryside while enjoying city life.

After reading the book on Shamanism, I downloaded a Shamanic drumming soundtrack, accompanied by a guided meditation. The risk of going into too much detail about my experience is to influence what you may or may not find should you attempt your own venture into the lower, middle or upper worlds associated with Shamanic journeying. Out of respect to the native cultures from where Shamanism stemmed, journeying isn't something that I regularly practice. Although it could be argued that all meditation is a form of journeying. The experience was profound, and it sits in my memory like an effervescent dream. What happened definitely happened, but once again, attempting to relay the experience with words is a pale shadow of the experience itself.

I lay a blanket beside my favorite tree in Richmond Park (I'd recently been talking with trees again, just like I used to when I walked to school as a kid), and lay back and listened to the guided meditation. I entered what is known as the Lower Realm by visualizing an opening in the tree, through which I climbed in and followed a path to a woodland in my consciousness. There I met my Animal Guide, and was taken through memories of childhood and certain instances when my Animal Guide was there to protect me and guide me. These memories came out of nowhere, particular moments when I had been or was about to be physically injured, or times when I needed the courage and strength to overcome daunting situations. I was shown that this Guardian had always stepped in, surrounding me with its strength and sometimes fury, yet all the while it sat with me during this vision, indifferent and cool. The experience was amazing. I thanked my Animal Guide for sharing this knowledge with me, and went through the process of leaving the same way I had come in, back to my blanket beside the tree in my mind's eye, and back to our physical world. I came around to regular consciousness as though waking from a trance, which I suppose is exactly what happened. I thanked my tree for the assistance and left, feeling excited and rejuvenated. I was equally amazed at how easy it had been. I've since learned that it's easiest for us to connect with our Animal Guides (Power Animal, Spirit Animal, Totem Animal, to use Shamanic and Neoshamanic names) than our other Guides, such as Ancestral or Ascended Masters. But this we will go into in more depth in the next book.

Some months later, after my mother had passed away, I attempted Shamanic Journeying once more, with a question for my Animal Guide. Specifically, I wanted to know how to develop my connection to Spirit, and in particular how to cultivate mediumistic abilities. I went through the process of listening to the drumming soundtrack, climbing down into the Lower World, and there my Animal Guide was waiting once more. Cool, calm, indifferent to my presence. I asked my question, and was given a single word answer. A word I'd never heard of before, a word I had no way of recognizing or knowing. It could be argued that the word was already stored in my memory somewhere, and that I simply plucked it out when it suited my purpose, but that truly wasn't the case. I received the word, left the Lower Realm, and came back to our Physical World. I immediately Googled the foreign language word that I had been given, I didn't know the language, I'd never heard this word before. When I had asked what I could do to improve my connection with Spirit and to develop the abilities of communicating with people on the Spirit Plane, I was given the Hindi word for "meditate", or "place of meditation". I found this to be truly remarkable, since Shamanism has its roots in Northern Asia, and meditation is the doorway to Spirit.

Chapter Fourteen

Caol áit

The term Thin Place is thought to come from pre-Christian Ireland. Caol áit, a Gaelic word (pronounced "kweel awtch"), refers to a place, often in nature, where the veil separating the Physical World and Spirit World becomes thin. Perhaps you have experienced a Thin Place when walking through a forest, or trekking up a mountainside. You may even have stumbled across one in an old house, or on an empty street at night. It is where the distinction between our world and the other momentarily disintegrates. They are places where your own Spirit suddenly tunes in and speaks up and lets you know that the past, the present, the ethereal, all blend into one and you just *know* that you're in a special place. I have experienced such places. The area where I discovered my favorite tree in Richmond Park is undeniably a Thin Place. It stopped me when I first wandered through it. I didn't even know about the term Thin Place until later on. Carisbrooke Castle on the Isle of Wight is another of my familiar Thin Places. A random pub in the UK once struck me as a Thin Place, where there was a shift in my awareness brought on by the place itself. You might have your own favorite Thin Place. A beach where you stared at the night sky and felt your Spirit expand and blend with the stars above. A new city where you'd never been before immediately felt like home when wandering its streets. A windswept cliff looking out over a turbulent sea. Or perhaps even your own back garden, where you've planted vegetables and read books undisturbed.

The Ancient Celts of Ireland, Scotland, Wales and England had a keen sense for such places. Our landscapes are covered with monuments, markings, and ruins that decipher such spots where the ancients had felt the fabric of reality gently tear to reveal a world beyond the world. In a quiet or perhaps reflective moment, we are able to feel the connection with the people who first marked these places, drawing our attention to them forever since. Places where Nature Spirits dwell (they are a thing) and time itself is vivid and tangible, making the past seem here with us, right now, and our connection to both the Spirit World and the physical world one and the same. As I always like to try and point out, the argument against this could be that we *think* Thin Places exist around castles, old houses, or places such as Stonehenge or the Ring of Brodgar, simply because they exist, and look mysterious. But I don't believe that is the case. I believe those places feel like Caol áit because that's what inspired our ancestors to mark those spots in the first place. Besides, oftentimes a Thin Place is nowhere near a monument or Neolithic structure. They can just as easily be an empty field or country lane.

One thing is for sure though, if you have already stumbled across your own Thin Place, then there is sometimes no better place to sit and connect with your Higher Self through meditation. Of course, if your Thin Place is frequented by tourists, then you might want to find another one!

For our next exercise, we're going to go a little deeper, and expand a little wider. This is going to set us up for the next part of the book which will begin to focus on mediumship, and connecting with our Spirit Guides. As I come to the part of what happened next in my own life, and what finally spurred me to answer what I believe is a call I ignored for far too long, we will concentrate more on meditation and awareness. I hope by now I have begun to open your awareness to your own deeper truth, through telling you about how I gradually found mine.

If you have a Thin Place in nature, then I implore you to practice this meditation whenever you next get the chance to go there. It isn't a prerequisite. This meditation works absolutely fine sitting in your bedroom or kitchen also. But there is something about being outdoors in nature which both helps to connect us to Spirit, and physically energizes us simultaneously.

Meditation Exercise: Taking Root and Letting Glow.
Level: Beginner

First, find a quiet space where you won't be disturbed for ten or fifteen minutes. This can be outside, at home, or wherever you feel safe and relaxed. Sit with your back straight, in a comfortable but not too soft chair. If you are outdoors, a bench or even laying down is also fine. I advise not laying down at home in case you end up nodding off.

Sit with your hands neutral, on your lap or on the armrests of the chair. Have your feet placed on the floor, take your socks off if you can.

Now, I want you to close your eyes and take a deep breath. Breathe through either your nose or your mouth, it doesn't matter which, just fill your lungs, then exhale. Close your eyes, and take another one, a big inhale, filling your lungs, feel your chest expand, and then breathe out and let it go.

Keep your eyes closed, and let your breath return to its natural rhythm. Take your concentration to your breath. Just be aware of it, don't worry about it, let it do what it's been doing your entire life. Let yourself breathe naturally and give it some of your attention.

You'll probably notice that your thoughts are doing what they usually do, and drifting from one thing to the next. And that is absolutely fine. Let them do what they do. And if you find yourself paying attention to any of them, simply remember your breath, and feel the air going in and out of your lungs. Cool on the intake, and warm on the out-breath. Those thoughts will soon get tired of trying to distract you, and they'll move along. Sure, there'll be another one right after them, but again, focus on your breath, the natural rhythm of your breath, harmonizing your body, in tune with your heartbeat.

Next, I want you to take note of your feet placed on the floor, and I want you to imagine tree-like roots sprouting up from the Earth, and into the soles of your feet. If you live on the tenth floor that's fine too. Imagine the roots traversing up through the building, up through the foundations and each floor, to connect you to the Earth herself.

Your roots begin soaking up the Earth's energy, and you feel it moving upwards, a glowing green light that travels up through the roots and into your feet, up past your ankles and into your calves. The light shines from your legs as it travels up, warming, cleansing, nurturing and healing. Earth green light that envelops your knees, and now up and around your thighs. Feel the energizing light as it travels around your groin and the base of your spine. Let it sit there for a moment, infusing the base of your spine with its healing energy. Feel the light there connecting you to the Earth as you begin to slowly pull the green light up around your lower back and navel area. Let it swirl around your torso and permeate into your abdomen with its soft, healing energy. Let it settle any discomfort you have there, and sit there for awhile, nourishing, healing, and warming. Feel the light sparkle outwards, just below your belly button.

Next, pull the green light up around your solar plexus. Part of your sympathetic nervous system is there, which takes care of your stomach, kidneys, and your liver. Let the healing Earth light sit in this area and work its magic, cleansing, restoring, activating, and then feel the light rise further, and up to your heart.

It is here that the light will truly glow, as it blends with your sacred heart energy and shines forth from your chest and out into the world. Your entire lower body, from your feet to your heart are now enveloped in warming, healing, green energy from the Earth. Let it stay with your heart, glowing with love, and spreading out around you, enveloping you in its soft healing haze.

Next, feel the light travel up through your chest and down your arms, all the way to your fingertips. Feel it clear any impurities in your lungs as it moves up to your throat. Feel it clear any blocked energy that resides in your throat area. Our voices vibrate from here, and it is important to heal this area if we are to speak our truth and be heard. The food we eat travels down here, and the air that we breathe. Let the light clear anything that is clogged in this area, any past arguments, anything left unsaid that should have been heard. Let the throat area open wide, and let the light shine forth from it.

Feel the light travel up and around the base of your skull, warming your face, and resting at your forehead. You already know that this is a very powerful spot. Let the light nourish this area, perhaps flashing indigo as it heals and opens and relaxes your forehead. Let it sit there awhile.

And now, let the light travel to the top of your head, feel it expand upwards and out, connecting you with the universe.

You are perfectly positioned between Heaven and Earth, open to the stars and grounded with the trees. Sit in this Power, feel the vibration of your body. Listen to your breath, and listen to your heart. Feel yourself glow. You are made of light, light from above and light drawn from the earth's energy below.

When you feel it's time, pull the energy back down from above and through the top of your head, closing off the connection and closing your Crown Chakra as the light comes back in.

Let it pass down through the forehead, closing your Third Eye as it goes.

Feel it travel around your throat, closing the Throat Chakra as it goes.

Feel it travel down through your chest, closing your Heart Chakra as it goes.

Let the light travel down past your Solar Plexus Chakra, closing it as it goes.

Feel it travel down and around your navel and back, closing your Sacral Chakra as it goes.

Feel the glowing green light travel around your groin and base of spine, closing your Root Chakra as it goes.

Feel the cleansing, energizing light travel down your thighs, healing your knees, warming your calves, travelling down through your ankles and down the roots from the soles of your feet and back down into the Earth. Feel the roots retract, as they move with the light and back to the Core.

Listen to your breath. Inhale deeply now, and as you do so, wiggle your toes and tap your feet.

Feel the chair that you sit on, or the ground, and move your fingers. Bring your chin to your chest and roll your head, and finally, open your eyes.

Welcome back.

Chapter Fifteen

Chakra

The Chakras are part of ancient esoteric beliefs originating in early traditions of Hinduism. The belief is that we exist both physically and non-physically simultaneously. What is referred to as the "subtle" body, exists energetically, while the physical body exists as a tangible solid mass. The subtle energetic body has multiple points of focus, which directly influence both the metaphysical mind and the physical body, and in turn affect our emotions, moods, karmic energies and ability to connect with our higher selves or Spirit. The most relevant Chakras exist in a line from the base of the spinal cord to the top of the head, in vertical channels. There are thought to be thousands of Chakra points, but the ones we mainly concentrate on are the seven principal portals that we were introduced to in the previous meditation. We will only briefly touch on them here. It is important to learn more about the Chakras before attempting to continually open and close them. Yoga classes, Reiki courses, or an experienced practicing medium will be able to teach you how to safely open and close your Chakras in a controlled environment. For the purpose of this book, and beginning to open ourselves up to Spirit, it isn't in any way dangerous to begin to explore the Chakras in meditation. But to delve deeper, I definitely recommend finding a book or teacher specializing solely on the subject.

The Root Chakra. Also known as the Base Chakra. It is located as the name suggests, aligned with the base of your spine. It is characterized by stability, self-sufficiency, a connectedness to the earth, and in grounding meditations. When the Root Chakra is balanced you will feel strong, confident, and grounded. It is often seen as the color red.

The Sacral Chakra. Located in alignment about two inches

below the navel. It is connected with sexuality, creativity, and self-worth. When the Sacral Chakra is balanced, you will feel compassionate, vibrant, satisfied and intuitive. It is associated with the color orange.

The Solar Plexus Chakra. Located between the navel and upper abdomen, it is concerned with our self-esteem and confidence. When imbalanced, it is thought to signify problems with digestion and liver issues. When balanced, you will be energetic, confident, and focused. It is known to be connected with the color yellow.

The Heart Chakra. When we open the Heart Chakra, we are able to send our love out into the world and use our own healing energy to help others. It represents love, compassion and empathy. When balanced, it connects us with others and keeps us caring, friendly, motivated and open to sending and receiving love. It is associated with the color green.

The Throat Chakra. Located at the base of the throat in line with the thyroid gland. When aligned, you are able to communicate freely and be understood, you will speak with compassion and know your words are true. You can communicate constructively and clearly. The Throat Chakra is known to be blue.

The Third Eye Chakra. Located between the eyebrows, a few inches in front of the head. Its attributes are intuition, intelligence, insight and awareness. When balanced, you will feel more connected to the Spiritual World and your Higher Self. You will trust your intuition and feel light and spiritually progressive. The Third Eye Chakra glows the color indigo.

The Crown Chakra. Located at the top of the head. The Crown Chakra connects us with Spirit, and the Higher Dimensions. When balanced, it brings us into awareness of cosmic consciousness. It frees us from our ego, and opens the channels to the constant flow of universal enlightenment.

The Crown Chakra is our connection to The All That Is, and is the color violet.

Chapter Sixteen

The Turning Point

Somewhere around the end of summer 2020, my life went into upheaval. Firstly, the flat that we rented was due to be renovated and sold. Even through COVID times, between lockdowns, our landlord made it clear that we should look for another place of residence. Around this same time, my mum began to grow increasingly confused. We would video chat three or four times a day, and it became apparent that she was struggling to recall things or have a coherent conversation. I immediately went to the island to see her. I had been avoiding going there through government lockdown rules, and it seemed likely that her confusion stemmed directly from spending so much time alone, and not leaving the house. She spent a few days in hospital while they ran tests to discover the root cause of her sudden confusion. Miraculously, she began to make fast improvements while she was there. We could hold a conversation again and she passed the doctors' memory tests, and they sent her home. But not before setting up a care package, where voluntary nurses would check in and dispense the multitude of medication she was on.

I decided at that point that COVID rules could go to hell, and I travelled down to the island weekly to check on her, as well as having our daily video calls.

Laura and I lived with some friends for awhile, but it didn't work out, and after two months we moved in with Laura's boss in Barnes, who kindly got us out of a pickle. She gave us an entire floor of her house to ourselves, which gave us some brief respite. The amount of stress at the time was overwhelming. Between my mother's health, having all of our belongings packed in storage, scraping by on money from the government since not being able to work due to the pandemic, moving home twice in two months, and last but not least, the state of the world due to COVID-19 itself, it was all getting a bit much. I'd resorted to my old friend alcohol once more, and was drinking on a near daily basis. All thoughts of Spirit Guides, meditation, auras and Chakras, were very, very far from my mind.

On one of my last visits to the Isle of Wight to see my mum, I took her for a short walk around the block. She hadn't been out in months, and she had slowed down immensely. For some reason I didn't comprehend how much her physical health had gone downhill. Her mind was back on track, and she still had the carers who would come to the house three times a day to give her her meds, but for all intents and purposes, she seemed like my old mum again. I suppose that due to us talking every day, I hadn't realized the state of her physical decline. It's very disappointing to me now, that I hadn't paid attention to it. I was so used to her bouncing back after various setbacks, I just assumed that this was another and that she'd be back to her old self shortly.

The very last time I physically saw her, restrictions had been eased and I thought it would do her good to get out for a few hours. I never stayed the night, because of government rules and the fear of giving her COVID, but we had a few hours in the afternoon and I took her to a local coffee shop that we used to go to. She really picked up. We ran into a few of her friends, and we had a nice couple of hours together. We made plans for her to come up to London for Christmas, and we were very much looking forward to it. We booked the hovercraft, and a taxi to bring her up in a week or so. It was December 15th, and that was the last time I ever physically spent time with her.

A new COVID variant hit our shores, and at the last minute, the government instructed us to cancel our Christmas plans. My mum was scared of travelling alone. There were all sorts of confusion regarding people being stopped at stations and ports and being told they couldn't travel, so we decided against her trip. Laura and I had an uneventful Christmas together. Naturally she missed her family in Finland, and I was disappointed that my mum couldn't spend Christmas with us. Laura and I spent the entire period in a half drunken state. On New Year's Eve we danced around the living room listening to 80s music. It was the first New Year's that my mum didn't call me at midnight. She always used to do that, no matter where I was in the world. When the clock struck midnight in the UK she would call, but this year she had an early night. There didn't really feel like there was much to celebrate.

The first couple of weeks of 2021 drifted by uneventfully. My mum was set to have her first vaccine jab mid-January. I'd also been booked on a new job, that was to start mid-January. Three to four months on a big Marvel superhero movie. While preparing for that, and because of the latest restrictions, I didn't go and visit my mum on the Isle of Wight.

The night before my mum passed, we had our last of probably three or four conversations of the day.

She would always leave her mobile phone charging in the hallway, just outside the living room door, on the floor plugged into the wall. She answered the FaceTime call, leaning over the phone as she went to pick it up, appearing in the bottom half of my screen. A man was leaning over from the other side of the screen also, an older man, with thinning grey hair, silver-framed spectacles, and a disposable surgical mask over his mouth, pulled just below his nose. It wasn't unusual to see someone else there, I assumed he was one of the voluntary nurses, although it was a little late for them. They would only pop in for ten minutes at a time, and their shift ended around 6pm. It was almost 9. I was also instantly annoyed that he wasn't wearing his mask properly. What was the point in me staying away and trying to keep her safe when these people, who visited multiple persons per day, couldn't even wear their protective gear correctly? I was about to give him a piece of my mind.

"Was that one of the carers?" I asked my mum, as she took the phone and sat down in the living room.

"Was what one of them?" my mum replied, settling herself into the sofa.

"Are the carers there right now?" I asked again, slightly taken aback.

"No," she replied. "They were here at dinnertime and being a bloody nuisance." She'd been complaining about them a lot over the previous weeks. She had essentially returned to normal, and felt that she didn't need "strangers coming in and making a mess of my house." She truly was back to her old self again. She knew what meds she should take (sometimes better than the nurses) and was preparing her own meals, eating properly, and watching her favorite TV shows. Whatever the confusion had been through the autumn due to months of isolation, she was over it.

Still, I had just seen someone, no doubt about it. So I questioned her again.

"Wait a minute, Mum," I said. "Sorry to interrupt. But are you telling me that there's absolutely no one with you in the house right now?"

"No," she replied again dismissively, and started chatting away about something else.

Well, I was completely baffled. It was a fairly small house, the front door was right next to the living room. I would have heard the door opening and closing if anyone left, and they would have said goodbye. No one visited her, she didn't have any male friends aside from Frank across the road, and the man I'd seen wasn't Frank. We spoke for about thirty minutes and there was absolutely no indication of anyone else being with her. She spoke freely and openly. I could always tell if there was a visitor when we talked on the telephone, her demeanor would completely change and she wouldn't act like herself. In fact it was a trait of hers that used to annoy me since I was a teenager. What's weirder still, is that I completely dismissed it.

I had pretty much ignored every sign throughout my life, that I was seeing glimpses into a realm that most people don't see. Even when I knew beyond a shadow of a doubt that I was experiencing such things. "Real" life would creep back in, and I would get caught up in the daily dramas of it all. Even when I'd been thrust out of it, when my mind could no longer comprehend the absurdity of time, or when I'd been labelled a mystic, or when I woke up knowing that something beyond this world was downloading me with information from a Higher Source, from seeing glowing grids to conversations with Animal Guides, I still dismissed a sign that a life-changing event was about to happen. That the person who I loved more than anyone else on the planet was about to leave. Someone was letting me know they were there to collect her, and I simply dismissed it.

Must have been mistaken. A trick of the light. A glitch on the screen. A reflection from the TV. None of these things were what I saw. I saw a man, an older man, with thinning grey hair, glasses, and a mask pulled just beneath his nose. Only for a couple of seconds, but long enough for me to note these features. Yet my brain told me that it was impossible, because there was obviously nobody else there.

Right at the end of the call I had an overwhelming urge to take a screenshot of my mum. She looked sad, she looked tired, she was wearing a cute fluffy red cardigan with gold-colored buttons. I suddenly really wanted to take a photo, but I thought it would have seemed an odd thing to do. She might have heard the camera shutter sound, or maybe her side of the call would have notified her of what I'd done, so I decided against it. We said I love you, and she said, "Goodnight. God-bless," like she'd said every night that we had ever talked since I was a child.

I went in to the living room and Laura asked me what had happened. How come I'd been questioning my mum about someone being in the house? I said I thought I'd seen someone, but I must have been mistaken. We went to bed that night and the next morning I was woken to a phone call that my mum was having a heart attack.

Chapter Seventeen

Grief

So who was he? A Spirit Doctor? My mother's Guide? My guess is he was my father. I haven't seen my dad since I was eighteen years old. Back then, he had one lung, smoked two packs of cigarettes a day, drank a couple bottles of whiskey a week, and worked on building sites from 5am until dusk. If he had made it to the year 2020 he'd have been around the same age as my mum, and I would imagine given his lifestyle he would have definitely been in the vulnerable category. I hadn't seen the man on the screen long enough to really take note of his features. Why was he wearing a mask? If we're talking ghosts here, why would a ghost be wearing a surgical mask? In solidarity due to COVID? Someone I later spoke with about this, on the set of the Marvel movie I was about to start filming, said that actually, maybe it was solidarity. Imagine if he hadn't been wearing a mask, in the middle of a pandemic. How would I have reacted then?

I'm certainly not a qualified councillor, and I don't have any official advice on grief. I can only tell you how I have handled my mum's passing and what has helped me. Pretty much everything that has been my life since my mother's physical death to this date, has been part of the grieving process. There's barely a minute in the day when I don't think of her. As I sit and write now, I am in her house on the Isle of Wight. Almost one year to the day since I last physically saw her. I have very mixed emotions about coming here. It's bittersweet. Even now, after all of the affirmations I have received since her death that she is still very much alive and aware of my life, I still cry. I cry every time I come to this house. I cry when I leave it. I cry at random TV commercials or songs, but I no longer cry as much as I did in those first months.

I started work a couple of days after my mum died. I wanted to stay busy. I can't say if it particularly helped or not, but I also needed money. When someone dies, and you are their survivor, a lot of bills tend to show up, not to mention funeral costs. So I had the Marvel movie to get on with. *Doctor Strange in the Multiverse of Madness*, the sequel to *Doctor Strange* and subsequent Marvel films about Spider-Man and Thor and the like.

(For any Marvel geeks out there, Wikipedia claims the movie took a break from filming from January to March, 2021. I can absolutely attest that it didn't.)

For the initial few weeks on *Doctor Strange*, I really struggled. I would talk to my mum in the mornings, on the way to catch the first train from Barnes to Longcross Studios. England was hit with a particularly vicious winter weather spell over those first few days. The streets were icy at 5am, when I would walk to the station. I would speak out loud to my mum, the same way I had every day on the phone. Sometimes I would even speak *into* my phone if I happened to pass another morning commuter, so they didn't think I was nuts. I would tell her about the film I was working on and what we were shooting and so on. I played a minor character in the film, and ordinarily I would have been semi-starstruck to be standing next to Benedict Cumberbatch in his full superhero regalia, but I barely noticed he was there. I kept to myself and didn't talk to anyone on set for the first month of filming. Between takes, I reread a book by Neale Donald Walsch titled *Home with God*. It helped. I would cry in the toilets at lunch. If I happened to get into a short conversation with another cast member, I would somehow turn the conversation to my mum's passing within the first few sentences. I went home late at night, would devour a bottle of wine before bed, then was up at 4 and walking to the station in the snow, talking out loud to my mum.

Somewhere during this period, Laura and I moved to our

own flat. A bright and modern apartment in the Burrough of Richmond upon Thames. Towards the end of shooting the *Doctor Strange* sequel, I began to open up a little to those around me, and by the end of March I had made a few solid friendships that continue to this day. I fell into conversation with a woman around thirty years old named Megan, who I would see most days, and she took the subject of my mother's passing to the esoteric.

"Why don't you ask for a sign?" she suggested.

"A sign?" I replied. Such a thing had oddly never crossed my mind.

"Next time you're home alone, simply ask your mum out loud to show you that she's still with you. You'll get a sign. I guarantee it."

The next day, I was sorting through my vast (and now obsolete, thanks to streaming services) collection of Blu-ray discs. I have a lot. Things were in boxes still, all around the apartment. But my Blu-ray collection were all together, and I placed them methodically in the drawers beneath the television and Blu-ray player. While doing this, Megan's words suddenly came back to me. Ask for a sign.

Despite talking to my mum every morning on the way to work, and telling her all about the film we were making, I found it a little awkward to do this. In fact, it wasn't awkwardness, it was fear. What if I asked and nothing happened? Likely, nothing *would* happen. I mean what *could* happen? So I blurted it out.

"Mum, if you're with me, can you give me a sign that you're around. It would help me so much. Thank you. I miss you. All the time. And I love you." Before I started choking up, I went back to the business of arranging my Blu-ray collection.

I continued putting them in order. I was afraid they wouldn't all fit in the two drawers beneath the TV. Eventually I got to my collection of Marvel films, and I started geekily putting them in order of release date. I thought I was all done, when I realized one was missing.

Doctor Strange.

Well how the hell can this be? I thought. They were all in the same box, every single one of them was there except for that one. And why *that* one? The movie that I was filming a sequel to! What were the chances? I started pacing around the apartment. Books were piled up on tables and clothes were strewn on the bed. Where on earth could it be? Every single Blu-ray disc was accounted for apart from that one.

And then I spotted it. Sitting on top of a pile of books, the other side of the room. Most of the books I hadn't read and had been meaning to get around to. I went over to pick it up and noticed the first name of the author of the book underneath it, one corner poking out beneath the *Doctor Strange* Blu-ray.

Maureen. My mum's name.

The corner of the book below that one was poking out also, revealing the first word of its title.

Living.

Chapter Eighteen

We Go On

My physical health took a downwards spiral, for the most part of 2021. Particularly during the first months after my mum transitioned from this world to the next. I began drinking heavily again. By the time we had her funeral in March (it took two months because of the sheer amount of deaths from COVID-19) I was polishing off three bottles of wine a night, all the while getting up at 4am to go and film the movie. But through all of the grief, through the daze of alcohol, through the constant flow of tears, I knew that my mum was still with me. In my heart of hearts, I could still feel her. Palpably. I could feel her in a way that I hadn't been able to feel her when she was alive.

I downloaded an audiobook by a medium called Claire Broad. The title of the book had caught my attention. *What the Dead are Dying to Teach Us*. Claire had experienced her first connection with Spirit while in Richmond Cemetery, visiting her grandfather's grave when she was a little girl. This resonated with me immediately since I had lived directly across the road from that cemetery, when we first moved to London. Claire could have been from anywhere in the world, for all I knew, but she had grown up right down the road. Her book helped me to deal with those first few months of grief. Her no-nonsense, matter-of-fact way of explaining all that she had learned from her connection with Spirit, peaked my interest in mediumship.

Spring arrived, and one afternoon while walking through Barnes, I stumbled across a small church, nestled back off the street, almost hidden from view. Barnes Healing Church. I read the notices on the bulletin board in its courtyard. Demonstration of platform mediumship, Sundays at 6.30pm.

I'd never heard of such a thing before, but it seemed pretty self-explanatory. I had only just finished reading Claire's book on being a medium when this church appeared. I'd walked down that street a handful of times, and never noticed the church before. I contacted the organizer via email and asked how the demonstration worked, and would I be able to attend. Before I did, I made sure that I set all of my Social Media accounts to private. I didn't want any unscrupulous charlatan discovering my recent loss prior to showing up to whatever this platform thing was.

A man named Eugene replied and explained that I simply needed to turn up on a Sunday evening, whenever I felt comfortable. No money would exchange hands. A medium would stand before the congregation and demonstrate mediumship. So the following Sunday I went along.

Janet Neville was the medium that evening, and she was there with Steve Bridger, a man who had transcribed her messages from Spirit into a book simply called, *Being Spirit*. Both were perhaps in their mid to late 50s, and after an introduction by Eugene, and then a few words from Steve, Janet stood on the platform. The church itself wasn't quite what I expected; in fact I was pleasantly surprised how it aesthetically blended tradition with a modern vibe. There was a picture of Jesus on one wall, and a large brass crucifix on the opposite side of the raised podium where Janet, Eugene, and Steve sat. It had a balcony decorated with fairy lights. When Janet stood to begin her demonstration, she seemed to be in a sort of trance. She was looking not at anyone in particular but beyond the fifteen or so of us that sat facing her on the church pews. After a few moments, she immediately turned her gaze to an elderly lady in the front row, and began talking about a cottage in Scotland. The lady confirmed that she knew of the cottage, and that it was where her husband had been brought up. Janet went on to give the lady further messages from her husband's family, talking about her husband's health (he was alive but not in attendance that evening) which all seemed to make absolute sense to the elderly lady.

Janet moved on to a young woman sat a few rows ahead of me. This time she claimed to be receiving messages from the woman's grandmother. I was in a skeptical frame of mind, almost feeling somewhat defensive, but the more Janet talked with people the more I began to realize it would be impossible for her to be so specific and correct if she were making it up, or "cold reading" people. Impossible. No one was giving any information to her other than yes or no answers. The young woman a few rows ahead of me confirmed that everything Janet was saying about her grandma was true.

Suddenly, Janet locked eyes with me.

"Hello," she smiled.

"Erm, hi," I replied.

"You alright?" she asked.

"Erm, yeah not bad," I said. A few people around the church let out a polite murmured laugh. I didn't realize it, but Janet was speaking to me as the Spirit who was coming through. She appeared to slip in and out of this state. Sometimes addressing me directly as the person in Spirit who was giving the messages, and sometimes talking as herself. She had a natural London, slightly Cockney accent, when she spoke as herself.

"I've got a young man here," she told me. "Who would have been in his forties if he was still alive. He doesn't want to tell me how he died."

I was instantly disappointed. I wanted to hear from my mum. What young man? And then I thought of Sami.

Sami was a Finnish friend of mine who I had worked with in Helsinki, who had tragically taken his own life in his early thirties. I haven't known that many people who have passed over, and only a few young men. It made sense that he would be in his forties at this point, since he was a couple of years younger than me.

"He's talking about his shoes," Janet went on. "He said you both wore a particular kind of uniform. Does that make sense?"

Alright, I thought, Sami and I worked at a nightclub together. We wore a casual uniform that we always would try and stray from, replacing the shirt with our own black T-shirts or tank tops, which needled the hell out of our boss. But there was no policy about footwear. That didn't really make sense. I nodded nevertheless.

"Yes or no please," Janet instructed me.

"Erm, yeah, I think so," I said.

"He's telling me now that you have important work to do. That one day you will be standing where I am. But you're still slightly skeptical about this whole thing."

That caught me off guard. Since reading Claire Broad's book, I had been looking at courses on learning mediumship. I hadn't told a single person about that, not even Laura. Especially not Laura. She might think I was nuts.

"OK. I mean yes. But I'm not skeptical, I do believe in this," I said.

"You have always known about life beyond life," she said, speaking as the Spirit now. "And you're finally ready to begin working as a Healer. You have incredible healing powers, and the gift to connect with Spirit. You've known this since you were young, and you tried to connect with Spirit when you were young."

Well this was weird. I thought of the Ouija board experiences from my teenage days.

"He's talking about his shoes again," Janet said. "He seems to think that's really important. Something about your shoes, or boots. You don't recognize him yet. He said you were the more serious one and he was always playing around. You took your studies more seriously than he did, when you went to college together."

Woah.

****ing woah.

She wasn't talking about Sami. It was Tom. Tom who I had gone to college with. Tom, who wore cowboy boots the same as me when we would be the odd ones out among our friends. Tom, who attempted to connect with Spirit with me using Ouija boards. And Tom, who had tragically died after falling in with the wrong crowd when he was only 21.

"I know who it is!" I blurted out.

"You see?" Janet smiled. "I knew we'd get there in the end." She continued to talk as Tom, about how I am a Lightworker and that I've finally found my path. That it will take time to develop my skills, that I'll grow impatient with an apparent lack of progress, but that I must stay focused and on the path. That in time I will be standing on a platform giving demonstrations of mediumship. Janet continued to talk and stress about how this was my calling, that I was surrounded by light, and that I must persevere.

As amazing as this was, and as I think about it now, it truly was humbling and positive and astounding all at the same time, I was still disappointed that my mum hadn't come through. Janet continued to talk about me becoming a Healer, and that my true calling in life was just beginning. But my mind drifted away a little. I missed my mum. So very much. I'd asked my mum to be there if she could hear me, in the days prior to that night. If she could hear me could she just let me know that she was alright.

Janet suddenly paused.

"I've got a lady with me that recently passed," she said. My heart began to race.

"She would have been in her mid to late seventies, does that make sense?"

"Yes," I quickly replied, feeling dizzy, my mouth going dry. "That makes sense."

"Emotion," Janet said. "*So much emotion.* She wants you to

know that she's alright, and that she was also alright when she passed over."

This had been something that had been plaguing me. When the firemen got into the house, since no ambulances were available, they had found my mum laying in the hallway at the bottom of the stairs. I had been terrified to ask if she'd fallen down the stairs, I couldn't bear the thought of it. The cause of death had been a heart attack, and the coroner's report listed nothing more than that. I'd settled with the idea that she was already downstairs when it happened.

Janet's accent suddenly switched from her London dialect to a Derbyshire accent.

"Angels came and lifted my body and carried me up, well, not my body but my Spirit, and oh it was wonderful," she said. My mum's voice, my mum's words and way of speaking and my mum's accent. A wave of relief washed over me.

"She wants you to know that she loves you," Janet said, her accent returning to her own. "And she's always with you. She's standing behind you right now, with her hands on your shoulders."

Although the message was brief, it was enough for now, and it helped me enormously.

Janet went on to talk to a lady behind me about her son's death. She went straight to it. There was no doubt in my mind by this point, that Janet was the real deal. No one would suggest someone had lost a child without being 100% certain. The lady confirmed everything Janet said, and seemed relieved beyond words as tears rolled down her face.

What I had experienced in that church was nothing short of amazing. I had no idea that such places even existed. Platform mediumship takes place in Spiritual Churches up and down the UK and across the world. I left that evening feeling elated and encouraged, and relieved. I had just listened to my mum speak, three months after she had died.

Of course, grief is still grief, and I still had a lot to deal with. I miss my mum every single day. I would give anything to have her back here, and as it approaches the year mark to her passing it grows increasingly hard. At the time of writing, Christmas is two weeks away, and I can't help but want to skip the entire thing. I understand that this is a natural reaction to such landmarks, and I believe that my mum is still with me and thriving more than she was when she was physically here, but it still hurts that I can't give her a hug. As I write this book, tomorrow is exactly one year from when I last gave her a hug.

Chapter Nineteen

The Clairs

The Clairs is a collective term relating to the different types of intuitive abilities that correspond with the metaphysical and spiritual senses. If you are unfamiliar with them, you probably have at least heard the term Clairvoyance, what is commonly referred to as the sixth sense. The four most common Clairs are: Clairvoyance (seeing people, places, objects or situations related to a person's present, past or future), Clairsentience (intuitively sensing, feeling the energy and emotion of a person or place, or the presence of someone passed on), Clairaudience (clear-hearing, being able to hear either in the mind or with your ears, someone who is in the Spirit Dimension), and Claircognizance (clear-knowing, similar to Clairsentience, but the ability to know the information you are receiving about a place, person or object is accurate and true). There are lesser known Clairs such as Clairgustance and Clairsense (tasting and smelling), Clairtangency (touching an object and receiving information about its past and owner), and Clairempathy (tuning in to the emotion of another person or someone who has passed over. This term is also used to describe the sensations a medium receives from someone in the Spirit World who might wish to convey they passed from a heart attack, or lived in a hot climate).

The terms are interesting, and at the beginning are useful tools to decipher where your abilities may lie when learning to tune in to your intuitive gifts. For example, I have so far experienced Clairsentience, Clairsense, and Clairtangency, and I suppose Clairvoyance also describes what I witnessed at the start of this book. But as you develop your intuitive abilities, I believe that simply going with the flow is all that's needed. If you suddenly and intuitively experience a deeper understanding of a situation that you are involved in, or while meditating you smell your grandma's cooking, or hear a voice from a deceased loved one, I don't personally believe it makes much difference whether you label it as Clair number 4 or 6. I'm only starting on this journey, and an accomplished medium might consider what I just wrote to be wrong. But I believe that rather than getting bogged down in the details, it is better to concentrate on quieting the mind and being open to receive whatever insight comes to you, regardless of which way it comes in.

As someone who is actively attempting to improve my own intuitive abilities, I can say with certainty that in the right state of mind, the first impressions that come to you are usually the correct ones. Before the brain gets a chance to catch up and analyze whatever it was that you gained insight to. Later on towards the end of this book, I'll give a few examples on how this has worked for me.

In my very first instances of receiving information from Spirit, it tended to happen immediately upon waking. Which makes sense. Right before the prefrontal cortex of the brain can distinguish between thoughts and decisions, an idea or knowing will come in. And I know it's not from me, and you will know it too when it happens to you. It's subtle, but it's definite. The thought is not yours, it's a communication. The same has happened while writing this book. When I've begun to flow and almost fall into a trance state. I've looked back on what I've written afterwards and known that what's on the page has come through me but wasn't authored by me. There's a difference in the style suddenly, the language will sound ever more slightly profound, the message being written will have nothing to do with me or my life as I've described it here and will be about the greater good. I've noticed that these few paragraphs will appear at the end of a chapter. After I've recited whatever my original idea was, there'll be a sudden insight. A few lines of wisdom that I don't remember writing when I've reviewed it later on. It's fascinating, and it gives me confidence that this book will make its way into your hands because that is for the greater good. It's not about me. I'm just a tool, a means to an end, and anything related to my life that I relay here is simply a vehicle to get the bigger messages across. There will be more of these books, and they'll be less about me and more about us, as a collective, as a whole, as a species moving forward in spiritual evolution.

Damn. I think it just happened again.

Let's get back to the Clairs, and I want to share with you an exercise that has helped me quiet the mind, and move towards deeper meditation. All you need is a candle, and a darkened room.

Meditation Exercise: The Flame. Level: Beginner

Take a single candle and something to light it with. Find a quiet space where you won't be disturbed for ten or fifteen minutes. Practically, this needs to be indoors. Draw the curtains if it is light outside, cut out most light pollution from everywhere that you can. Turn your phone face down and silence it, or preferably turn it off all together for the duration of what we're about to do. Light the candle and place it firmly at eye level in front of where you are about to sit, a few feet in front of you. Obviously, ensure that the candle isn't near anything flammable or likely to fall over. Sit with your back straight, in a comfortable but not too soft chair, with your feet firmly planted on the floor.

Now, I want you to close your eyes and take a deep breath. Through either your nose or your mouth is absolutely fine, just fill your lungs, then slowly exhale. Do this once or twice and then let your breath return to its normal pace.

Look at the candle.

Don't concentrate on it intently. Just be aware of its presence. Feel free to stare at it, watch the flame dance and change color and form, but look away every now and then. It's there, but it's not the be and end all of what you are doing. Spend a couple of minutes glancing at the candle, let your eyes wander around the darkened room, stare back at the candle for awhile, etc.

Now close your eyes and watch the light that has left its impression on your retina. It floats behind your eyelids and changes color and shape, and it moves around as your eyes drift relaxed in your head. Don't worry too much about pulling it back into place. Just watch it, changing color and shape. Watch it for as long as it is there. And I'll leave it with you. Something wonderful might happen.

After the exercise, brighten up the room, snuff out the candle, and go and do something mundane such as making a sandwich or a cup of coffee.

Chapter Twenty

The Visitor

Within days of going to the Spiritualist Church, I noticed a workshop coming up at the London College of Psychic Studies. The college was formed nearly a century and a half ago, evolving from the London Spiritualist Alliance which started in 1883. Sir Arthur Conan Doyle, creator and writer of the *Sherlock Holmes* books, *The Lost World*, and others, became president of the college in 1925, and bought the location for its current headquarters at Queensberry Place, Kensington.

Claire Broad, the author of *What the Dead are Dying to Teach Us*, was holding a day workshop at the college during the Spring of 2021, and I quickly signed myself up.

Claire opened the class with a meditation. I was getting used to meditating now, since I would listen to a guided meditation most days, either at home or in Richmond Park. But something happened during this meditation that had never happened in others. Within minutes, I felt myself begin to vibrate and grow dizzy. That same sensation from all those years ago when I had dabbled with the Ouija board, and when I had awoken one morning to what I described as a download of information, and saw the glowing holographic grid. I felt myself swoon and feared I would pass out in front of the class of twenty or so people in attendance. So I quickly cut it short and grounded myself, and went through the guided meditation without fully embracing it. I don't know what would have happened if I'd simply let go, but being as this was my first class, I was afraid to jump in at the deep end.

Claire talked about Spirit, her Spirit Guide, and how the process works for her. She took us through a few exercises on how to connect with Spirit ourselves, and paired us with other members of the class to try and practice and hone our own abilities. In all honesty, despite learning a lot and enjoying the class immensely, I didn't experience anything or receive any insight from the Spirit World. Others in the class seemed to have varying success with their own attempts. During the lunch hour, I chatted with Claire and told her about some of the experiences I've already described in this book. For once, I wasn't met with awkward averted eyes or an instant dismissal of the things I described. Claire explained to me that the Crown Chakra, located at the top of our heads, is our most powerful connection to Spirit. It's where we communicate with the Divine, the Collective Consciousness of the Universe, and the Spiritual World. It's where we receive guidance and wisdom, and she told me it makes sense that I experienced a sensation of a stream of information shooting directly into the top of my head when I had awoken one morning to the sight of a glowing grid. When this happened, I'd known nothing of a Crown Chakra at all. I also told her about what doctors had described as psychosis, when I felt completely trapped in the moment of now, and began to view time as a spiral, rather than linear. Again, she knew exactly what I was talking about, and compared it to what Eckhart Tolle had gone through in order for him to write the best-selling book *The Power of Now*.

"It looks like they're really trying to get your attention," Claire told me at the end of the class. "Will you keep in touch? I'd be interested to hear about your progress."

I went home that night feeling that I'd actually been taken seriously by someone, when talking of my incorporeal experiences. It was reassuring and encouraging, and that night I continued to focus on meditation. In fact, I'd been meditating daily for that whole week. Laura was in Finland, visiting her family, so I'd taken the time to try and reboot myself both physically and mentally. I'd been hitting the gym every day, meditating, taking long walks through Richmond Park, eating healthily and abstaining from alcohol. I went to bed the night of Claire's class feeling clearheaded and balanced. I climbed in with a book, the cat jumped up and settled next to me, and then all of a sudden, the atmosphere changed.

I couldn't tell you how I knew it had changed, I just knew. The cat had also noticed it since she was suddenly sitting upright and staring into the corner of the room, close to the head of the bed.

"You noticed that too, huh?" I said to the cat, who continued to ignore me and stare into the top corner of the room.

Now, anyone who's got a pet knows that they are prone to looking at things which aren't apparent to us. Cats, in particular, are easily distracted by shadows, lights, bugs, pretty much anything that sends them into hunting mode, and I've seen her do that a hundred times. This was different. She wasn't staring at any moving reflections of light or floating dust. In fact, absolutely nothing stirred in the room at all, other than the sense that the atmosphere had most definitely changed. Beyond the big sliding doors of the balcony, sits the very flat, very wide roof of the offices below. There's no light pollution from the street, no head beams of passing cars make it up to our floor, and besides, the blinds were fully drawn closed.

After a few minutes of staring up at the top corner of the room, up to the right of my pillow, the cat suddenly jumped down off the bed and went over to the same corner, looking up. She sat down, arched her head upwards, and stared at the wall.

"Mum?" I asked quietly to the room.

I stayed perfectly still, watching the cat stare into the corner. I suddenly had the inspired idea that I should capture what was happening, and took my phone from the nightstand beside me and hit record.

The cat sat unmoving for eight more minutes, staring up at the same spot a few feet from the head of the bed to my right. After eight minutes, she suddenly stood and walked away, as though a spell had been broken, and wandered off across the room. I continued to record the empty space, slowly moving the camera around the dimly-lit area. The only light in the room came from the diffuse lamp to the side of me, which cast a warm orange glow around the bed.

If someone is with me, could you please show me that you're here?

I asked this question in my head rather than out loud. Since researching mediumship for a few months, I'd learned that communication comes through thought and feeling, rather than the need to vocalize our words.

Mum, if you're with me, please show me in some way that I could recognize.

No sooner had I put this thought out, something wonderful happened.

A glowing ball of light swiftly and gently appeared from beneath the bed and circled around a clotheshorse standing full of T-shirts and socks. It hovered in midair for a moment, before zigzagging back and forth and shooting upwards leaving a fluorescent white trail, and then vanishing completely.

"Oh wow... wow..." is all you can hear me gasping on the video.

I recorded the entire moment.

I felt nothing but love, I felt nothing but peace, and I went to sleep that night knowing that we are never, ever alone.

Chapter Twenty-One

The Skeptics

I've always found it difficult to put into words, those things about which we are delving into here, things that I intrinsically, always knew. If I can go back to that day with my friend when we were children once more, the whole "I am me" thing, I knew that he hadn't grasped what I was saying. And over the years I would grow frustrated with friends who failed to see or care about things that I found of vital importance simply because we exist and are here. I remember in a nightclub one evening, arrogantly and drunkenly telling my girlfriend and a male friend about how they couldn't possibly understand what I was talking about because they were still asleep. I was frustrated. And another evening, asking an old school friend about what she thought was beyond our planet, out in the universe.

"Space," she replied.

"But what's beyond that?" I asked her.

"Nothing. It's just space."

"But what was before space? What caused the so-called Big Bang?"

"Well there wasn't anything before the Big Bang," she replied.

The problem with trying to have these conversations, is that sooner or later you hit a brick wall. We all do. Whether you work for NASA or Uber, we all eventually come to the same conclusion.

We just don't know.

Let's go back to that old chestnut, my old nemesis, time. The greatest scientific minds on the planet can't agree on what time itself actually is. Newton's Realism. Galilean Relativity. Einstein's Relativity. Gödel's Incompleteness Theorem. St. Augustine, after pointing out that he was able to talk about time without knowing what it was, wrote in *The Confessions*, "I do not even know what I do not know."

That was in AD 430. And we still don't know.

So when something that we are faced with all day every day, that dictates our lives, that divides our years, ultimately makes little sense, what hope do we have in explaining personal, ethereal experiences to someone who hasn't had them? We simply can't fully comprehend such experiences because they don't happen within the realms of the logical brain. They happen somewhere else. They happen at a super-conscious level. They happen with knowing. And that is all.

After seeing the Orb float around my room, after capturing it on camera, I excitedly rushed to show the video to one of my best friends.

I watched him watch it with eager anticipation about what he would say. But instead of telling me that what he just witnessed was amazing, that it now showed him beyond a shadow of a doubt that there is more to this life than the physical, he began questioning it. Could it have been a reflection of the phone? How did he know that there was no light coming in from the window since he hadn't been there? He couldn't give his approval for sure, he said.

I was deflated. I felt like telling him that he should know because I told him so. We're best friends. What possible reason did I have to trick him? I was sharing something with him that had happened, and what had happened was amazing. I wasn't asking for his validation. I simply wanted him to see it. What were the chances? Was it simply a random weird fluke of light that zigzagged around the room, and left a trail behind it when it shot off? And that happened the very same day that I'd spent meditating in a class attempting to open up to Spirit? The second that I asked for a sign it appeared, and I was recording an empty room because I *knew* that something was different. I'm not in the habit of laying in bed recording the bedroom with my phone before I sleep. Coincidence?

I very quickly decided that it's not my position to convince people of these things. You can talk about your experiences, but until people have them, they can't truly understand.

And I get it, I do. I doubted a call to action for years. Repeatedly. In writing this book and going over all of the signs I received, it seems obvious that something was trying to get my attention. But I didn't see it at the time. It took my mother passing for me to wake up.

You are a Lightworker. If you didn't know that already, let me assure you that there is no question about it, since you've made it this far through this book. But the trick is to let the ego subside, and let the Light shine through you. It's not about you, or me, or convincing someone else that you know better because of the experiences you've had. We are here to be guides along the path. If someone doesn't see things like we do, all we can do is carry on, and be the Light that leads the way.

We are each on our own individual journey, and despite a huge shift in consciousness on the planet, and many people opening up and being willing to have conversations about the spiritual, there are still many who have little interest in exploring the subject and are happy to march complacently forward. Tell them about your own journey, but don't expect everyone to agree, understand, or even care. It is frustrating and it *does* feel like a shame, but all we can do is evolve at our own pace.

As I've mentioned already, my partner Laura has always been skeptical, since having an intensely religious upbringing, and rejecting those ideals and theologies. She always compared any talk of a Creator to a religious version of God. She believes in evolution and nature, and without meaning to patronize her, it's only been lately that she's coming around to the idea that I believe the same as her. We just use different words. Everything is energy, and as little as a few weeks ago at the time of writing, we shared an experience together that was familiar to me but completely new to her.

We both had the day off work. I had been slacking with my meditation practice for a few days, and so I asked Laura if she'd like to join me in a guided meditation. She agreed, and I found a fairly short one on YouTube from the medium Gordon Smith. It was one of the first guided meditations I had done, almost a year before, when I first started practicing opening up to Spirit. We went through the meditation together, and I found it hard to completely give myself over to it since I was wondering how the experience was for Laura. I was also aware that some of the language Gordon used, about opening up to Spirit and bringing in Spirit Guides, might be a bit too abstract for her usually analytical mind. Regardless, we did the meditation, and then headed to the city for a meal. As the evening drew in, we wandered into a pub in Soho. We hadn't been to that pub before, and Laura went to the bar to get us a couple of drinks while I secured us a table and two stools. It was one of those very old school, old-fashioned styled English boozers with small upholstered stools, carpet on the floor, and card beermats on the tables. Laura sat down and no sooner had we sipped our drinks than something shifted in the atmosphere around us.

The pub was fairly busy, there were people at the bar and sitting at the tables beside us, but what happened next was purely between the two of us.

"You feel that right?" I asked Laura.

"What's happening?" she asked me, looking elated.

"I'm not sure, but this is what I've been telling you about."

We both felt a wave of energy wash over us, and it stayed with us, letting us know that it was there. A presence. A glow. Someone, wanting us to know that we had company. I'd immediately known that Laura could feel it, and I knew that she knew that I felt it too. It was a warm, loving energy, and it continued to pass between the both of us, pulsating, strong, invisible, but undeniably there.

"You see now, right?" I asked her.

"I don't know what to say," Laura replied, still looking amazed. "I have no words for what I'm feeling. I don't know what's going on." Her eyes were wide as she analyzed whatever it was that was happening.

"This is it, this is what I've been saying," I struggled to explain it to the both of us. "It'll pass soon, and we won't remember it properly. That's why I want you to describe what you're feeling. It's amazing, isn't it?"

I could already feel the energy beginning to dissipate.

"I'm already losing it," I said.

"I can still feel it," Laura told me. "I just don't know how to explain what's going on. I feel safe, I feel excited."

I attempted to try and help Laura to stay in the moment, to soak it up and to hopefully remember it when it passed. After perhaps another minute, Laura said it had left her too, and the sounds of the pub started creeping back in. We were back to where we'd started a few minutes before.

"I don't know what just happened," Laura told me.

"Something was letting us know that it was with us," I said. "I've felt this kind of thing before, but I'm amazed that you felt it too. I didn't know that could happen."

Laura began to describe what she'd been feeling, only moments before, and struggled to recollect.

"This type of thing," I went on. "It doesn't sit in the memory the same way as everything else does. It's a different type of knowing. It presents itself to you but in a different way than the five senses. You feel it. You know when it happens. But you can't remember it in the same way as you remember other things, or describe it after."

I was so excited that she'd experienced something like this. But as quickly as it had arrived, it had now completely gone, with little trace but a fragmented memory.

The next day, I contacted Claire Broad, who I now considered a friend as well as a teacher. I'd done another workshop with Claire, a wonderful one in the autumn, where I'd seen a glowing golden angel wing stretch out from the side of one of my classmates. We'd meditated, connected with Spirit, and amazing things took place over the three-day course. I'd given correct readings to some of my peers, told them things about their deceased relatives that I couldn't have possibly known, and been told by Claire and a developing medium that they could see a direct and strong link with Spirit emanating from my Crown Chakra.

"It's possible that you picked up on an entity that resides at the pub," Claire had said, when I told her about our experience. "Maybe it was checking in with you both and letting you know that it was there. But my guess would be it was one of your Guides. Since you'd both meditated that day for the first time together, they love that. When two people who love one another reach out, there's no way that was a coincidence that this happened on the same day."

What's amazing to me still, is that we both experienced it. Laura, a self-proclaimed agnostic, went through the exact same thing that I did at the same time. We have of course talked about it since, and neither of us can now put into words exactly what happened. Through my studies, I've also learnt that on very rare occasions, a person in close proximity to a medium might hear what the medium hears, when Sitting In The Power. They can tune into the energy that the medium is channeling. But I truly believe Laura is a sensitive, like myself. I believe that Spirit linked with her as well as me and wanted to give us both a little welcoming gift. For as long as we've been together, Laura's intuition has always been on point. Better than my own. But her beliefs have so far kept her from exploring any esoteric avenues. I can't and wouldn't want to enforce my beliefs on her, but after that experience, and the countless times I've told her about my own, I'd like to think that she's coming around a little bit. If I could put a wink emoji right there, then I would. And just to conclude this chapter, I'm also reminded of the experience that both myself and my friend Tom went through together when we were teenagers. For me it continued for months, but for him it had only been that one time, when we had been together after attempting to blindly and haphazardly connect with Spirit using a Ouija board.

Chapter Twenty-Two

Spirit Guides

According to Wikipedia, some Spirit Guides are persons who have lived many former lifetimes, paid their karmic debts, and advanced beyond a need to reincarnate. Many Spiritualists believe that Spirit Guides are chosen on "the other side" by human beings who are about to incarnate into this life, and are assisted by these chosen Guides throughout their earthbound lifetime.

One of my teachers and fellow Richmonder, Yamile Yemoonyah, authored the award-winning book *The Seven Types of Spirit Guide*. In it, she lists the archetypal Guides that we may encounter when opening ourselves up to Spirit. She also talks about how Spirit Guides aren't necessarily only deceased people who once walked on the earth, and what different global cultures believe. Spirit Guides can be Animal Guides, Nature Spirits, Star Beings, Ancestral Guides, and other incarnations. I met my own Animal Guide in 2020, prior to diving headlong into mysticism and a full year before having any idea about writing this book.

Spirit Guides are there to inspire us, to direct us, and occasionally to warn us. Some may refer to their input as intuition, that gut feeling which guides us in uncertain situations. Sometimes their voice is loud and clear, others it's a gentle tug to steer us towards a better version of the future. If I ever doubted the existence of such beings before, I definitely don't anymore.

A medium is assisted by her Spirit Guide when connecting with deceased loved ones, on behalf of a client. A Spirit Guide will act as a mediator, and will bring in the Spirit who wants to connect with the medium and pass on a message. The Guide can protect the medium from being overwhelmed when he opens himself up to the Spirit World, and keep those wishing to relay a message in an orderly queue. Traditionally, a medium will first connect with their Guide, and the Guide will bring them the Spirits who wish to converse with the living. You may have already met your own Guide, but as of writing, I am still going through the process of connecting with mine. In a workshop, a friendly, traditional-looking Buddha appeared to me, floating in my mind's eye in a sitting position. He wasn't there long; he appeared to me and smiled, then vanished. Also, in deep meditation, I saw a turbulent sea with fleets of ancient wooden ships. A god-like warrior stood at the bow of one of them, with flowing hair and braided beard. I believe that he was my Deity Guide, and that he has come through again when I received information about him from another medium. During the development circle that I attend, my teacher, Gilly, told me that I have an Ascended Master Guide, who was a Jewish jeweler when he was in the physical world, and that he's with me through most of my day-to-day living. I met my Animal Guide right at the beginning of my journey already, in a very powerful, very real vision during meditation. Our Guides aren't there to answer our every whim, or even our prayers. They don't work for us, but they do work with us. It takes time to establish a connection, and I am still at the very beginning of my journey.

One evening, while visiting my mother's house on the Isle of Wight, about eight months after she had passed, I had become increasingly distraught and very caught up in a deep envelope of grief. Sometimes visiting the house was therapeutic for me, others I was overwhelmed with sadness, mostly it would be both. The smell of the house would always be the first thing that hit me when walking in. Next would be the memories, and next would be the silence. On this particular evening, about six months in to my exploration of opening up to Spirit, I was attempting to receive a sign from either my mum or my

Guides. I'd spent two days writing this book while there, and meditating intermittently. I had been taking long walks through the countryside, and doing everything I could to see some sort of confirmation that what I was doing was correct, that I was on the right path, and that Spirit was indeed with me. On the second evening, the night before I was going to head back to London, I hadn't experienced anything. No vision during meditating, no flickering lights, no sense of someone being close by, no flashes of inspiration or messages. I took a late night walk to the beach and was growing increasingly upset and frustrated. I was doing everything right, I thought. I was attending the Spiritualist Church, I had started writing a book about my progress, I was meditating daily. I was devouring every book, every television show, every workshop I could afford about opening up to Spirit and developing intuitive abilities. Sure enough, I had received an undeniable message and proof that my mum still exists from the medium Janet Neville, and it had been life changing. I'd had another affirmation when the Orb danced around my room. But I wanted another. And I was growing angry that I wasn't being rewarded with a direct message from my Guides (this was prior to the visions I received later on, or the experience that Laura and I shared in the pub).

It was nighttime, and I walked in floods of tears along the beach esplanade. Barely anyone else was around. There were a few fishermen lined up on the beach, facing the sea with their rods dug into the sand, their lines cast out into the darkness. I all but collapsed beside a beach cafe, placed my head in my hands and continued to sob. I missed my mum, so, so much. It hurt. Despite knowing that there is more to life than what we experience daily, it still hurt. She still wasn't physically here. I never got to say goodbye. Where were my goddamn Guides that I was attempting to contact every single day? Why weren't they answering? Why didn't they help? I began shouting out loud through my tears. My face was flooded with salt and mucus and

I was a pure mess.

"What's the point in all this?!" I yelled into the night at my Guides. "What's the big ****ing secret?! Why is this life set up like this!? If I know that you're out there and I'm supposed to be connecting to you, then why don't you show up?! Why do we have to go through this process of pain to get to the truth?! What *more* do you want me to do?!" I went on and on, shouting and wailing and aware that the fishermen dotted along the sea's edge further down the beach could probably hear me and probably thought I was a lunatic.

"Why don't you answer me??!!!" I screamed in anger, before once again burying my head in my hands and letting it all flow.

After awhile, something told me to look up and to my left, to the beach cafe that was beside me on the sand. It had a chalkboard on its wooden wall, probably for the day's specials, but instead of soup and sandwich prices, it looked like some kids had scrawled something all over it. I couldn't believe what I saw. You might not believe it either.

"Phill." Written in white chalk. And then all around my name, it said, "Hi."

```
hi hi hi hi hi hi hi Hi hi hi hi
Hi hi    hi  hi HI   hi hi       hi hi hi
     Hi
          Phill


Hi hi
          Hi hi hi hi hi  hi HI  HI  HI hi
  hi  hi hi hi
     hi hi hi hi Hi hi hi
```

I started laughing, between the sobs. Was it really true? I pulled out my telephone and took a picture of the board. Amazing. Beyond amazing. A direct answer to my pleas. How more direct could it be? It was too surreal. It was what I'd asked for, plain and simple. My Guides were saying hi to me. Now, do I believe that a piece of chalk had magically written my name and 45 greetings all over the board while I sat there and cried? Probably not. But I do believe my Guides had predicted my plight, and taken me there to where the answer would be. The idea of a coincidence is more unbelievable than what actually took place, as far as I'm concerned. Maybe some kids had written it earlier in the day. Maybe one of them was called Phill. Or maybe my Guides wrote it. Our Guides are with us. And they are with us to do just that: Guide. We can't demand their help. They're giving it anyway. But we need to attune to their frequency if we want to make contact. I don't recommend getting angry and screaming on a beach. I was lucky to get an answer in the way that I did. But they are sending us signs all day long. As contrived as it sounds, look for the moments of apparent serendipity throughout the day. The song on the radio, the message from a friend you were just thinking about, the dream you had last night, that billboard ad that oddly had a slogan that answered your dilemma. Your Guides are with you. Through meditation and intention, you can meet them, and that's where we'll go in book two as I get to know my own.

Chapter Twenty-Three

The Drains

I've made mistakes. Many. I've done things I am not proud of. Repeatedly. We can't correct the wrongs we've committed in our lives, but we can try not to repeat them. As recently as a few hours ago, I got caught out on something I considered to be a minor wrongdoing, something that wasn't really hurting anyone, something that I was putting off taking care of due to other areas of my life taking over. And then I was faced with it.

There seems to be a pattern emerging, on this journey I've chosen to take. Things come up that I would have rather ignored. The past has come back, and made me face some uncomfortable aspects of how I once lived. It would seem that when we commit to this spiritual process, there comes a purge. If we are to be of service to each other, then we need to face our own shortcomings to move forward. It makes sense, and I am seeing proof of it in my own life on an uncomfortably regular basis.

There also comes another aspect to this process. In attempting to increase our awareness and openness to Spirit, we grow ever more sensitive in other areas of our lives. I can barely watch certain television commercials without bursting into tears. True, I am very much still going through the grieving process, but there seems to be a commonality among other people I have met along the way. We become highly sensitive as we begin to open up. When you reach the point in life where you want to develop your own spirituality, you are usually at a place where you know you no longer want to be. You know what serves you, and what does not. You know what you must do, to live a life of sincerity and honesty, and unfortunately, there are usually some casualties in your extended circles of relationships. There may even be some in your immediate one. And there will definitely be sacrifices to some aspects of your own personality.

People you know, will find it difficult to accept the change that they'll see in you. Particularly people who expect you to behave a certain way and respond to them in ways that they are used to. When you come to the point where you no longer see the sense in engaging in conflict, some will find it a tough pill to swallow. You won't respond the way you used to, you won't get triggered the way you used to. You'll only feel empathy, and want to help that person away from their own toxic energy. You will also notice those people who sap *your* energy. It may not be their fault, there may be depression involved, or other mental illness (and believe me, I am the last person who would casually disregard anyone's mental illness), but you will become aware that due to an increase in your own sensitivity, what you could once accept as tolerable behavior may become more difficult to align with, since you are now a sponge that is sucking in energy from every direction. A good friend of mine, who runs her own very successful spirituality-based business, calls this "The Drains".

There are ways to prepare and protect yourself from this, which can be as simple as meditating on positivity and light, which we have covered in the exercises in this book. But for now, I want you to bring your awareness to what I say next, because it will arise as you move on.

In attempting to connect with our Higher Self, let alone Spirit Guides or deceased loved ones, we have no choice to but reflect on what serves the greater good and what does not. There's nowhere to hide. You're either in or you're out. To come from a place of love, determines what you will bring to the table. You might get hurt, particularly if you are trying to make a change to a broken relationship pattern that no longer serves you. People will attempt to hold you back, and they may even remind you of who you used to be. But once you have made the decision to walk a spiritual path, there really is no turning back.

You don't need me to tell you this, you know as I have known when it happened to me. There will be some people who are not willing to accept your new direction. Particularly if they are people who you may have hurt in the past.

But as brutally honest with yourself as you will be forced to be, you must also remember, to be kind. You'll be kind to others, that's already a given. You can't embark on this quest without developing empathy for all living beings. But you must remember to also be kind to you.

We make mistakes, and you may have made many in the past. But that is not who you are anymore. All you can do is acknowledge your mistakes, apologize for them if possible, seek to make amends if it is appropriate to do so, and at the end of the day, you have to live with you. You cannot undo what has been done, but you must learn to live with it. You know your own truth now, and you know that you are trying to be better. You wouldn't have made it this far through this book if you were not. If someone cannot accept an apology, or refuses to let you move on from a past error, then you may have to consider regretfully letting that person go. What is for you won't go by you, and what no longer serves you no longer serves the greater good, for that is what you are working on now. Equally, you must not lose sight of your own well-being. Don't get so caught up in trying to help others that you forget to help yourself. Learn to forgive yourself. You deserve it.

Chapter Twenty-Four

Spiritual Warriors

As well as coming to terms with any uncomfortable personal obstacles you will have to overcome, you must also look out for not delving so deep into the supernatural that you lose sight of your everyday reality. I've fallen into this trap, and it is very easy to do. As your interest in the esoteric deepens, and your natural gifts develop, it can be tempting to get lost in the spiritual at the expense of the physical. We are, after all, still having a physical experience here, and we must not neglect it.

Over this past year, I have been witness to so many wonderful occurrences and affirmations that there is no longer any doubt in my mind that there is more to this life than meets the eye. I have accounted for most of them in this book. But there have been moments when I have had to step back and reconnect with the mundane. I found myself devouring every physical and audio book to do with spiritual growth that I could get my hands on. I was visiting my local Spiritual Church whenever a platform medium was giving a display, I was meeting with different mediums one to one, I was attending my development circle, taking weekly online classes, going to weekend workshops, and meditating on a daily basis. All of this practice absolutely increased my sensitivity and intuition and connection with my Higher Self. There came a point where I was seeing so many flashes of light around the house that I was considering getting my eyes checked! In the midst of my busiest explorations into developing my intuitive gifts, I was constantly seeing lights around me and out of the corner of my eye, especially right before bed. I made a conscious decision to step back, and no sooner had I done that than some instant dramas suddenly unfolded in my everyday life. Money became tight, work dried up, friends were in crisis, and I was forced to pay attention to my practical commitments. The flashing lights stopped immediately. It was as though I had flipped a switch and returned to what many people call the "real world". And what I concentrated on became my reality.

Balance. Balance is needed in everything, and as exciting as this journey can be, we must remember not to neglect our physical obligations and duties as part of society.

Another thing to look out for, are what I call Spiritual Warriors. These are people who have the greatest intentions, but oftentimes lack any discipline or direction. Now, I'm not professing to be an expert in the realms of the spiritual. I am no better qualified than any of us, and I am relatively new to taking this path consciously and committedly. But be wary of those who talk the talk yet don't walk the walk. I have witnessed firsthand rudeness, defensiveness, anger, conspiratorial claims and grudge-bearing from people who present themselves as enlightened. There seems to be a type, and I reserve judgement on anyone posting inspirational quotes on Instagram (nothing wrong with that in itself) while making a side hustle from promoting the latest holistic diet and making sure that everyone knows they're going to Burning Man this year. There is no wrong or right way to raising our vibration. We are each on our own path, and personally, mine has not been a peaceful one. The aforementioned "type" may be at the beginning of theirs, and we must not attempt to impede anyone expressing who they are. But one thing is certain, you will not belittle or be abusive towards another soul when you find the path. You will not bear grudges or seek vengeance for a wrongdoing. You will see each mistake and each injustice as a lesson learned and no more, and you will seek the bigger outcome from such occurrences. It takes time, but it is an inevitable by-product of spiritual growth. As the Internet and social media further connects us all, there appears to be a trend of conspiracy theories, lack of faith in government, victim-blaming, and ableism running rampant through self-proclaimed spiritually enlightened social-media gurus. We all have a right to our opinions, and we all have a right to grow spiritually. But choose your mentors wisely. They won't be seeking approval through likes on their social feeds. It is not about being perfect, or avoiding challenges. Have healthy boundaries and recognize your own needs as well as helping and caring for others where you can. Follow the journey with compassion and above all honesty, and love. There is no end goal. If I am learning anything along the way it is that there truly is no end, there is nowhere to get to. Death does not exist, and we will forever evolve and create ourselves anew in each incarnation of ourselves whether that be physically here on earth or when we continually cross over and come back and even when we cross over and stay. We make mistakes. We get lost. But we must wake up the next day and try again. Find your own truth. You'll know it when you do because you cannot lie to yourself. It's impossible. As I stated when talking about owning our past mistakes, you have to live with you. And this journey will ensure that you deal with yourself whether you like it or not. You cannot be a light unto the world if you are harboring darkness. Intention is everything. And that applies to all areas of your life. Intention breeds creation. Intention *is* everything.

Chapter Twenty-Five

Raise Vibration

As of writing, today marks the one-year anniversary of my mother's transition from the physical to the purely spiritual. I mentioned already that I would finish this book on this day; I believe my Guides let it be known. I also know that it will be at midday. I haven't aimed for this day, neither consciously nor, I believe, unconsciously. Throughout the last month and as this new year began I have written on random occasions, sometimes for hours and sometimes not for a week. But here we are, writing what I believe to be the final passage of this book before I revise, edit, and eventually publish. I have learned a lot through the process of writing this, about things I had forgotten, and things that seemed to happen *because* I've been writing this. One such example came when I wrote the passage about the last time I spoke with my mum on the phone. I wrote it sat at her kitchen table, in the house that I grew up in and still currently have the deeds to. I wrote about the mysterious face I had seen on the FaceTime call, the man wearing the mask who may or may not have been my father. A few hours went by after I wrote that. I wrote all night, and went on to the next passages about grief, and going to the Spiritualist Church for the first time. When I was done writing for the night, sometime close to midnight, I leaned back in my chair and revised what I had written. The house was silent and still, when all of a sudden, a smell appeared from nowhere that caught me completely off guard. I recognized it instantly, that I instinctively blurted out "Dad" before I even realized I was speaking. It was a scent that I hadn't smelled in nearly forty years, but it was unmistakable, it was *his* scent. The scent of aftershave mixed with steel and sweat, cigarettes and a slight trace of alcohol. It was his smell when as a kid I would run and jump and greet him when he came home from his work of managing a steel plant in middle England. I would bury my face in his neck and squeeze him tight. There is no other smell like it, and when you know it, you know. That night at the kitchen table, I had already moved on from musing over the chapter about the visitor with my mum on our FaceTime call, and whether it was my dad or not. But he came to let me know that it had been him, I have no doubt. It's hard to believe that it was a year ago last night when I saw his apparition with my mum. It's even harder to accept that I completely ignored it and denied what I'd seen and racked it up to my imagination. If I'd have been where I am right now in my intuitive development, I would have driven through the night and caught the first ferry to the Isle of Wight.

There have been other things that could be classed as paranormal activity that I have witnessed this past year, which I haven't included in this book. Lights switching on, a fan waking me up in the middle of the night in my mum's house that hadn't been on when I went to bed, and others. Things like this are not scary in the slightest. I am relieved, and feel lucky to experience them. They are affirmations that we go on, that we aren't simply made of physical matter. Love is as intangible as Spirit but we know it, and still feel the connection with our loved ones after one of us ceases to physically exist. Scientifically, we are more energy than matter. Each atom holds 0.001% matter, and the rest is energy in the spaces between, vibrating and blending with the energies from our friends and family, and even strangers who we encounter each day. That is the part of us that connects with Spirit. That is intuition, that is, to be taught from within. To know before thinking.

I've had several mediums tell me that I will become a medium. As of writing, that isn't my intention, but maybe it's inevitable. I do seek to expand my awareness, to raise my vibration, to develop my intuition, to be able to offer healing to those who need it, to connect with my Higher Self and to connect with Spirit. It's funny, writing that makes me realize I just described a medium. But I am only at the start of this journey, and in writing this book I don't claim to know any more than I have already shared. I am officially new to this, but I realize I've been connected to Spirit my entire life, and for the most part ignored it. If this resonates with you, then I hope that in sharing my personal journey, and my grief, it has in some way helped you with yours.

I am still learning the language of Spirit. In only my second development class last year, I attempted to read for a lady I was sat beside, a complete stranger to me. She handed me a small purse, and asked me what I saw. Immediately I had a flash of an old picture of my mother, a black and white photo of her from before I was born. She was at work, wearing a telephonist headset, sat in front of a board full of switches and dials, from when she used to work for British Telecom. She loved that job. But what did this have to do with my sitter's purse that she'd handed to me? Probably nothing, I thought. I was getting mixed up in my own hopes of someone in the class connecting with my mum. I mumbled something about seeing a wedding ring which made no sense to either myself or the lady I was attempting to read for. I was just making stuff up. After we were done, I mentioned how I'd seen the photo of my mum in my mind's eye. She smiled and told me that the purse she had given me was her own mother's, who was now in Spirit. She used to work as a telephonist for British Telecom.

The same day I attempted another reading for a young lady who, again, I had never met before. This time I saw one of my favorite old pubs on the Isle of Wight, a beach pub right on the sand, with fishing boats moored beside it, called The Fisherman's Cottage. What had this got to do with her? This was my thing, I thought. Next I saw a china tea-set and a fireplace. I relayed these things to her, thinking that once again my brain was showing me random stuff that had nothing to do with her. She told me that both of her grandparents were in Spirit, and her grandmother would ready the hot tea every afternoon beside the fireplace for when her husband came home from work. He was a fisherman.

It's early days for me, but I feel my connection is strong. Next for me is to increase that strength, and decipher this new language of Spirit. I shall continue to relay this journey for anyone who wishes to take it with me, and we shall learn together along the way. We all have the gift, but not everyone chooses to strengthen it, or indeed even acknowledge it (which was my case for so long), and some don't even believe in it. Life will unfold regardless of whether you live a life of intent, or if you choose to acknowledge that there are things beyond our understanding that serve our purpose of spiritual evolution. Intention is everything. Our loved ones walk with us and are whispering in our ear. We just need to quieten our minds and listen. My blessing to you and your journey. Raise your vibration, and glow.

Phill Webster
Richmond upon Thames. 14th January 2022. 11.54am

O-BOOKS

SPIRITUALITY

O is a symbol of the world, of oneness and unity; this eye
represents knowledge and insight. We publish titles on general
spirituality and living a spiritual life. We aim to inform and help
you on your own journey in this life.
If you have enjoyed this book, why not tell other readers by
posting a review on your preferred book site?

Recent bestsellers from O-Books are:

Heart of Tantric Sex
Diana Richardson
Revealing Eastern secrets of deep love and intimacy to Western
couples.
Paperback: 978-1-90381-637-0 ebook: 978-1-84694-637-0

Crystal Prescriptions
The A-Z guide to over 1,200 symptoms and their healing crystals
Judy Hall
The first in the popular series of eight books, this handy little
guide is packed as tight as a pill-bottle with crystal remedies for
ailments.
Paperback: 978-1-90504-740-6 ebook: 978-1-84694-629-5

Take Me To Truth
Undoing the Ego
Nouk Sanchez, Tomas Vieira
The best-selling step-by-step book on shedding the Ego, using the teachings of *A Course In Miracles*.
Paperback: 978-1-84694-050-7 ebook: 978-1-84694-654-7

The 7 Myths about Love...Actually!
The Journey from your HEAD to the HEART of your SOUL
Mike George
Smashes all the myths about LOVE.
Paperback: 978-1-84694-288-4 ebook: 978-1-84694-682-0

The Holy Spirit's Interpretation of the New Testament
A Course in Understanding and Acceptance
Regina Dawn Akers
Following on from the strength of *A Course In Miracles*, NTI teaches us how to experience the love and oneness of God.
Paperback: 978-1-84694-085-9 ebook: 978-1-78099-083-5

The Message of A Course In Miracles
A translation of the Text in plain language
Elizabeth A. Cronkhite
A translation of *A Course In Miracles* into plain, everyday language for anyone seeking inner peace. The companion volume, *Practicing A Course In Miracles*, offers practical lessons and mentoring.
Paperback: 978-1-84694-319-5 ebook: 978-1-84694-642-4

Your Simple Path
Find Happiness in every step
Ian Tucker
A guide to helping us reconnect with what is really important in
our lives.
Paperback: 978-1-78279-349-6 ebook: 978-1-78279-348-9

365 Days of Wisdom
Daily Messages To Inspire You Through The Year
Dadi Janki
Daily messages which cool the mind, warm the heart and guide
you along your journey.
Paperback: 978-1-84694-863-3 ebook: 978-1-84694-864-0

Body of Wisdom
Women's Spiritual Power and How it Serves
Hilary Hart
Bringing together the dreams and experiences of women across
the world with today's most visionary spiritual teachers.
Paperback: 978-1-78099-696-7 ebook: 978-1-78099-695-0

Dying to Be Free
From Enforced Secrecy to Near Death to True Transformation
Hannah Robinson
After an unexpected accident and near-death experience, Hannah
Robinson found herself radically transforming her life, while a
remarkable new insight altered her relationship with her father, a
practising Catholic priest.
Paperback: 978-1-78535-254-6 ebook: 978-1-78535-255-3

The Ecology of the Soul
A Manual of Peace, Power and Personal Growth for Real People
in the Real World
Aidan Walker
Balance your own inner Ecology of the Soul to regain your
natural state of peace, power and wellbeing.
Paperback: 978-1-78279-850-7 ebook: 978-1-78279-849-1

Not I, Not other than I
The Life and Teachings of Russel Williams
Steve Taylor, Russel Williams
The miraculous life and inspiring teachings of one of the World's
greatest living Sages.
Paperback: 978-1-78279-729-6 ebook: 978-1-78279-728-9

On the Other Side of Love
A woman's unconventional journey towards wisdom
Muriel Maufroy
When life has lost all meaning, what do you do?
Paperback: 978-1-78535-281-2 ebook: 978-1-78535-282-9

Practicing A Course In Miracles
A translation of the Workbook in plain language, with
mentor's notes
Elizabeth A. Cronkhite
The practical second and third volumes of The Plain-Language
A Course In Miracles.
Paperback: 978-1-84694-403-1 ebook: 978-1-78099-072-9

Quantum Bliss
The Quantum Mechanics of Happiness, Abundance, and Health
George S. Mentz
Quantum Bliss is the breakthrough summary of success and
spirituality secrets that customers have been waiting for.
Paperback: 978-1-78535-203-4 ebook: 978-1-78535-204-1

The Upside Down Mountain
Mags MacKean
A must-read for anyone weary of chasing success and happiness
– one woman's inspirational journey swapping the uphill slog for
the downhill slope.
Paperback: 978-1-78535-171-6 ebook: 978-1-78535-172-3

Your Personal Tuning Fork
The Endocrine System
Deborah Bates
Discover your body's health secret, the endocrine system, and
'twang' your way to sustainable health!
Paperback: 978-1-84694-503-8 ebook: 978-1-78099-697-4

Readers of ebooks can buy or view any of these bestsellers by
clicking on the live link in the title. Most titles are published
in paperback and as an ebook. Paperbacks are available in
traditional bookshops. Both print and ebook formats are
available online.
Find more titles and sign up to our readers' newsletter at
http://www.johnhuntpublishing.com/mind-body-spirit
Follow us on Facebook at https://www.facebook.com/OBooks/
and Twitter at https://twitter.com/obooks